Judaism in a Nutshell

An Easy-to-use Guide
For People Who Are Long on Curiosity
But Short on Time

by Shimon Apisdorf

LEVIATHAN PRESS
BOOKS THAT MAKE A DIFFERENCE

Judaism in a Nutshell: Israel
by Shimon Apisdorf

Copyright © 2002 Shimon Apisdorf & Judaica Press
First printing: June 2002
Second printing: January 2003
Third printing: August 2003

ISBN 1-881927-25-3

Cover design by Staiman Design
Page layout by Zisi Berkowitz
Research assistant: Dan Green
Technical consultants: E.R./D.L./Y.B.Z./B.C.
Edited and proofing by Sharon Goldinger, Nachum Shapiro
    and Rena Joseph

**Distributed to the trade by Biblio: www.bibliodistribution.com
Distributed to Judaica stores by Judaica Press: (800) 972-6201 or
www.judaicapress.com**

All books from Leviathan Press are available at bulk order discounts for educational, promotional and fund raising purposes. For information call (800) 538-4284.

Printed in the United States of America

ACKNOWLEDGEMENTS

Rabbi Michel and Rebbetzin Feige Twerski, Rabbi Noach Weinberg, Rabbi Menachem Goldberger, Bill Hackney, Yigal Segal, Dan Green, Aron Raskas, Andrea Schulman, Brian Applestein, Aryeh Mezei, Nachum Shapiro, Rabbi Asher Resnick, Hillel Soclof, Menachem Even Israel, Rabbi Reuven Green, Jerry Kiewe, Dov Mizrachi, Yitzchak and Debbie Fund & family, Sanford & Eppie Shore and Itchie Lowenbraun.

SPECIAL THANKS

My parents. David and Bernice Apisdorf.

Mr. and Mrs. Robert and Charlotte Rothenburg.

Esther Rivka, Ditzah Leah, Yitzchak Ben Zion, and Baruch Chananya.

Miriam. This is your book. Your love of the land of Israel, your incomparable editorial skills, and your whole-hearted readiness to support my often ridiculous writing schedule are what made this book possible.

DEDICATION

This book is dedicated to the memory of my Uncle Al, a man who loved Israel; Dr. Bill Eisner, a man who loved people; and Miss Goldie Lurie, a woman who loved life. It is particularly dedicated to the thousands of victims of Palestinian terror who were murdered and injured for only one reason—because they were Jews living in Israel.

Hakadosh Baruch Hu, source of all blessing

ISRAEL is the third volume in the
JUDAISM IN A NUTSHELL SERIES
Judaism in a Nutshell is one of many innovative, educational projects made possible by the Jewish Literacy Foundation

Jewish Literacy Foundation

17 WARREN ROAD SUITE 18   PIKESVILLE, MD 21208
(410) 602-1020   1-877-J-LITERACY
WWW.JEWISHLITERACY.ORG   INFO@JEWISHLITERACY.ORG

This printing of

Judaism In A Nutshell: Israel

has been made possible

through the generosity of

Barry and Sindy Liben

and their family.

We thank them

for their support!

Jewish Literacy Foundation

table of
contents

introduction

From Today Until Yesterday

Adolph Eichmann and Israel

In 1960, Israeli secret service agents located Adolph Eichmann in Argentina. In a short time he was captured and secretly whisked away to Israel where he was tried and eventually hanged.

The Eichmann trial raised a very basic question for Israel: What gave it the right to try Adolph Eichmann for crimes that had not been committed against Israelis, and had not been committed on Israeli soil, but which were in fact committed before a country called Israel even existed? Adolph Eichmann was the mastermind behind the deaths of millions of Europeans on European soil—his crimes had nothing to do with Israel... or did they?

The Eichmann trial brought into sharp focus the underlying meaning of the State of Israel, and the relationship of the Jewish people to the land of Israel. In the case of Adolph Eichmann, the world just seemed to understand the truth—that Eichmann's crimes were committed against Jews, and not Poles, Hungarians and other Europeans who "happened to be Jewish." Eichmann was a central figure in a plot that was as calculated, sophisticated, and modern as it was diabolical, barbarian, and evil. He had meticulously implemented Hitler's plan to destroy the Jewish people, and they had almost succeeded.

The country called Israel is much more than the national home of the Israeli people. It is the embodiment of the Jewish people. Israel tried, convicted, and hanged Eichmann not for crimes against Israelis but for crimes against the Jewish people. The country called Israel, in a way unlike any other country on earth, represents far more than just its citizens. It represents the Jewish people: past, present, and future.

Israel: *The* Land

This book is about the history of a country called Israel. Like all countries, Israel is a nation of people and cities, with its own economy, resources and politics, and with a particular geography. But there is more to Israel than all of these, for these are just the body, and Israel has a soul. It is impossible to fully appreciate the history of Israel without an awareness of its soul—its relationship to the Jewish people. It is for this reason that the story of Israel the country, and Israel the land, is also the story of Israel the people.

The vernacular in Israel today regarding one's place of residence divides the world into two regions: *ba'aretz*, "in the land," and *chutz l'aretz*, "outside of the land." Find Israel on a map of the world and you will see that it is so small that the printed names of many of its cities are too big to fit into the country itself, and so they kind of float in the Mediterranean or overlap other countries. If you were to superimpose a map of Israel onto a map of the United States it would show that two Israels could fit into the state of Massachusetts, nine into Ohio, and fifteen into California. Nonetheless, when Israelis look at a map of the entire world, they see only two places, Israel and outside of Israel. Why do I suspect that Icelanders don't look at the world in terms of two regions—in Iceland or outside of Iceland?

The notion that Israel is somehow an all-encompassing point of reference harkens back to the dawn of Jewish history. Throughout the Torah (the Five Books of Moses), Israel is invariably referred to in one of two ways. Either it is "the land of Canaan" or it is simply "the land." *The land of Canaan* is a geographical reference point. *The land* is a spiritual reference point. Geographically or politically, the land may be known as Canaan, Judea, the Levant, Palestine, or Israel. Spiritually it is *the* land par excellence—the only place in the world perfectly suited to the Jewish people, Jewish spirituality, and the Jewish mission.

The history of Israel, then, is more than the history of a country— it is the history of *the land*—that special place that is the heartbeat, the focus, and the soul of the Jewish people.

Abraham, Mesopotamia, and a Promised Land

The story of Israel is an example of history in the extreme. On the one hand, it encompasses the story—the history—of much of the world. On the other hand, it is the story of a tiny people and its relationship to a minute bit of the world's real estate. This book will tell the story of Israel in all its extremes. It will tell the story of much of world history as it unfolded in a theater called Israel—often on a stage called Jerusalem—and it will tell the story of the Jewish people and its relationship to the land called Israel.

All of these extremes can be found in the life of one man who lived in Mesopotamia some 3,670 odd years ago. The man's name was

Abraham, and he just happens to have been the first Jew to ever step foot in the land of Israel. So it is with Abraham that we will begin our story of Israel.

Abraham grew up in the great city of Ur in Mesopotamia. There, he was exposed to a culture unlike anything that had ever existed before in human history. In Mesopotamia, there were skilled craftsman of all kinds, people who could read and write, an elite cosmopolitan class, and of course an elaborate religious structure. Of all things Mesopotamian, Abraham just couldn't buy the religious beliefs. Despite the fact that he had been raised in a society that knew nothing other than polytheism, it all seemed like nonsense to Abraham. In time, Abraham did more than reject the belief system of his family, friends, and society—he came to a novel and utterly unique conclusion about life. Today we call that conclusion monotheism, the belief in one supreme God who is the sole source of all existence and upon whom everything remains totally dependent. It is at this point of radical departure that the Bible tells us that God appeared to Abraham, confirmed his convictions, told him to pack his bags, and sent him on his first trip to Israel, known then as Canaan.

> *"And God said to Abraham, 'Go for yourself; away from your land, the place of your birth and your father's house, to the land that I will show you. And I will make you into a great nation, and bless you, and you will be a blessing...' And Abraham took Sarai his wife... and they departed for the land of Canaan, and came to the land of Canaan. And God appeared to Abraham and said, 'To your descendants will I give this land...'"*
>
> Genesis 12:1-8

> *"On that day God sealed a covenant with Abraham, saying, 'To your descendants have I given this land, from the river of Egypt, to the great river, the Euphrates river.'"*
>
> Genesis 15:18

It is at this point, at a relatively early period in the history of civilization, that the relationship of the Jewish people—Abraham's descendants—to the land of Israel begins. We are now going to look at the lives of the patriarchs, Abraham, Isaac, and Jacob. It is these three men, together with their wives and children, that set the cornerstone of Jewish peoplehood, history, and destiny in place. With each, the most seminal events of their lives took place in the land of Israel, and one of them, Isaac, lived his entire life without ever leaving Israel. Let's take a look.

the promised
Land

I

those were the *Days*

1

It All Happened in Israel

If ever there was a people with deep roots, it's the Jewish people, and those roots can be found in the land of Israel. Almost every seminal event in the formative years of the Jewish people took place in the land of Israel. Whether God was promising Abraham that his descendants would be as numerous as the stars, informing Sarah that she would finally give birth to a child, or looking on while Jacob wrestled with an angel—it all happened in Israel.

Think of the rest of this chapter as early Jewish history in a nutshell.

From Abraham to Jacob, the Journey to Israel

The lives of the men and women who were the founders of the Jewish people were profoundly interwoven with the land of Israel. Abraham's first encounter with God was in the form of a command to go to Israel. There, an eternal covenant would be sealed between Abraham and God, a covenant that included the promise of the land of Israel to Abraham's descendants. Later in his life, Abraham and Isaac would be sent by God on another journey, this time to Jerusalem,

The Patriarchs in Israel

Event	Biblical Locale	Today	Year
Abraham			
Arrives in Israel	Shechem	Nablus	c. 1738 B.C.E.
God promises land to descendants	Shechem	Nablus	c. 1738 B.C.E.
Builds altar / teaches about God	Beit El	Beit El	c. 1738 B.C.E.
Blessed by King Malchizedek	Shalem	Jerusalem	c. 1738 B.C.E.
Sarah dies	Kiryat Arba	Hebron	c. 1676 B.C.E.
Abraham dies; buried by Isaac	Machpelah Cave	Hebron	c. 1638 B.C.E.
Isaac			
Sarah gives birth to Isaac	Beersheva	Beersheba	c. 1713 B.C.E.
Isaac is nearly sacrificed	Mt. Moriah	Temple Mount	c. 1676 B.C.E.
Isaac buried alongside wife Rivka	Machpelah Cave	Hebron	c. 1533 B.C.E.
Jacob			
Dream of the ladder	Beth El	Temple Mount	c. 1590 B.C.E.
Returns to Israel / wrestles angel	Jabbok river	Nahar Ez'zereq	c. 1554 B.C.E.
His daughter Dina is abducted	Shechem	Nablus	c. 1554 B.C.E.
Rachel dies and is buried	Efrat Road	Bethlehem	c. 1554 B.C.E.
Jacob dies in Egypt and is buried	Machpelah Cave	Hebron	c. 1505 B.C.E.

where the near sacrifice of Isaac would take place on what would later become the Temple Mount. Later, on the road to Bethlehem, the matriarch Rachel would be brought to her final resting place—a place that is still visited daily by Jews as a place of prayer and reflection. Then, years after the passing of Rachel, Jacob himself would be taken on his final journey—a journey from Egypt to Hebron—where he would be laid to rest along with his father and grandfather in the Machpelah Cave.

The Jewish nation's formative era began with Abraham's journey to Israel and concluded with Jacob's final journey, again to the land of Israel. Journeys to Israel, journeys with deep spiritual meaning for future generations, were bookends for the lives of the patriarchs and their families. Even after their passing, as early Jewish history moved into its next great phase, the journey to Israel would continue as a defining theme in the life of the Jewish nation.

An Egyptian Detour

For two hundred years after the passing of Jacob, Jewish history took a bit of a detour. This is the story of the detour: Abraham had a son named Isaac, Isaac had a son named Jacob, and Jacob had twelve sons (the twelve tribes of Israel), one of whom was Joseph. One thing led to another and soon the brothers were selling Joseph to a caravan of merchants headed for Egypt. Joseph possessed a magnetic personality and a knack for interpreting dreams. Before long, he was appointed to be the right-hand man to Pharaoh himself.

Seven years after the rags-to-riches rise of Joseph in Egypt, a devastating famine hit the entire region, including Canaan, where Jacob and his family lived. Thanks to Joseph, Egypt had stockpiled huge quantities of food and was able to sell surplus grain to others. In time, Jacob sent his sons to make a purchase in Egypt where they got more than they bargained for, including a dramatic reunion with their brother Joseph. Eventually, Joseph had his family settled comfortably in the Egyptian suburb of Goshen. Later, at the end of his life, Joseph would make one last request of his family.

> *"Joseph said to his brothers, 'I am about to die, but God will remember you and eventually take you to the land that he swore to Abraham, to Isaac, and to Jacob.' Then Joseph made the children of Israel swear, and said, 'You must bring my*

bones with you out of here.'"

Genesis 50:24-25

Not long after Joseph's death, a new Pharaoh raised the specter of dual loyalty, and soon the Jews were reduced to being brutally oppressed slave laborers. Despite seemingly endless years of suffering, the Jews knew that one day they would return to the land of Israel, and that they would take the remains of Joseph with them. When God appeared to Moses at the burning bush and informed him that the time for the Exodus had come, He made it very clear that their final destination would be none other than the land of their fathers.

> *"And God said [to Moses], 'I have seen the affliction of My people in Egypt. I will bring them up from that land to a good and broad land, a land flowing with milk and honey, to the place of the Canaanite.'"*

Exodus 3:7-8

And when the moment of freedom was finally at hand, the promise to Joseph was kept.

> *"And Moses took the bones of Joseph with him."*

Exodus 13:19

The moment of the Exodus from Egypt was the beginning of two journeys. For Joseph, it was a final journey home to be buried in the city of Shechem, known today as Nablus. For the newly liberated Jewish nation, it was the beginning of a journey to the land of their forefathers—the promised land of Israel.

David, Goliath, Hebron and Jerusalem

Forty years after the Exodus from Egypt, in the year 1273 B.C.E., the Jewish people, under the leadership of Joshua, crossed the Jordan River and entered the land of Israel.

> *"God said to Joshua, 'Moses has died. Now you and the entire people should get up and cross the Jordan and enter the land that I am giving to the Children of Israel. Be strong and courageous, because you are the one who will enable the people*

to settle the land that I promised to their forefathers.'"

Joshua 1:1-6

Fourteen years after crossing the Jordan, the conquest of the land and its division amongst the twelve tribes of Israel was complete. The next three hundred years are known as the period of the Judges, and featured people like Deborah—a wise and charismatic leader; Samson, of Samson and Delilah fame; and the prophet Samuel. During the era of the Judges, the government in Israel was decentralized, and the Jews frequently had to confront hostile neighbors, the most relentless of whom were the Philistines. The prophet Samuel was the last of the Judges, a man who commanded widespread respect amongst the people, and the person who became the bridge from the era of the Judges to a full-fledged monarchy. At the end of his life, the people prevailed upon Samuel to institute a formal monarchy. Before his death, Samuel anointed Saul as the first king of Israel.

The Philistines continued to harass the Jews during the reign of Saul. Against all odds, a young man named David met Goliath, the Philistines' most fearsome warrior, on the field of battle, emerged victorious, and became a hero. Eventually, David became the second king of Israel. Around 1000 B.C.E., he established his first capital in Hebron. Seven years later, he moved the capital to Jerusalem, which became the Jewish people's political and spiritual center for the next eight hundred years. It was under David's son, Solomon, that the First Temple was built on what is today known as the Temple Mount.

In the Blink Of An Eye:
Eight Hundred Years and Two Temples

The construction of the Temple was Solomon's crowning achievement, though it wasn't his only one. Under Solomon, the country experienced remarkable growth and development and Jerusalem became a city of international renown. The good times, however, did not last long.

Following Solomon's rule, Jewish national unity frayed until the country was divided into two competing kingdoms: The southern kingdom of Judah, whose kings were descendants of King David, and the northern kingdom of Israel, which was populated by ten of the twelve tribes. In the year 558 B.C.E., the kingdom of Israel was conquered by the Assyrians and the ten tribes were exiled and forever lost to Jewish history. About a hundred and thirty years later, the kingdom of Judah fell to the Babylonians. In the year 423 B.C.E.*, Jerusalem and the First Temple went up in flames.

The Jews that survived the Babylonian conquest were taken in chains to Babylon. Eventually, Babylon itself was conquered by the mighty Persian empire. It was under the Persian king Achashverosh that the events of Purim took place. Darius, the son of Achashverosh, eventually granted the Jews of Persia permission to return to Israel and rebuild the Temple. Though the Jews had achieved acceptance in Persian society and had built a thriving community there, an initial 50,000 people uprooted themselves to return home and build the Second Temple.

The period of the Second Temple lasted for four hundred rocky years. Only a few decades after the Second Temple was built, Alexander the Great arrived in Jerusalem and the Jewish state became part of the Greek Empire. The arrival of the Greeks set the stage for one of history's great epic struggles: the battle between Hellenism and Judaism. The confrontation came to a head in the year 165 B.C.E., when the Maccabees (under the leadership of the Hasmonean family) led a successful revolt against the Greeks. This triumph is celebrated today with the holiday of Chanukah.

Following the defeat of the Greeks, the Hasmoneans reestablished an independent Jewish kingdom, which lasted until the arrival of the Romans. In the year 63 B.C.E., the Roman general Pompey transformed Judea (as Israel was then called) into a semi-autonomous state under Roman administration. In 40 B.C.E., Rome installed a non-Jew, Herod, as king of the Jews. Though Herod was never genuinely embraced by the Jews, he nevertheless went to great lengths to build up the country. In addition to numerous public buildings including aqueducts, theatres, luxurious palaces and even new cities, Herod undertook to glorify the Temple as never before. Under Herod, the Second Temple became one of the marvels of the ancient world. The Western Wall, or *Kotel Ha'maravi*, that stands today in Jerusalem is a remnant of Herod's Second Temple. Herod's massive building projects, however, were matched only by his massive ego. He became a vicious and tyrannical ruler.

Relations between the Jews and Rome continued uneasily, and in the year 66 C.E., the Jews openly revolted against Rome. The revolt

---

* There is a dispute among historians regarding the date of the First Temple's destruction. You may be more familiar with a different date, 586 B.C.E.

ended in disaster in 70 C.E., with the destruction of Jerusalem, the burning of the Second Temple, the slaughter of hundreds of thousands of Jews, and the exile of those who remained.

The era of the two Temples had spanned eight hundred years and brought the Jewish people face to face with every great empire in the ancient world. That the Jews were able not only to survive those centuries but to thrive as a people was an extraordinary feat. Following the destruction of the Second Temple and the second exile of the Jews from their homeland, the Jewish people began a nineteen-century journey that became the most remarkable story in the history of mankind. Somehow the Jewish people survived nineteen hundred years of exile, dispersion, expulsion and brutal persecution. Then, as if in a deliberate attempt to defy all reasonable expectations, in the twentieth century, the Jewish people set out to reestablish sovereignty in their ancient homeland. In 1948, with the birth of the modern State of Israel, the impossible occurred. Once again, the Jewish people were sovereign in the land of their forefathers, the land of Israel.

Historical Overview Part I

From Abraham to the Spanish Expulsion
The first three thousand years of
Jewish History in the Land of Israel

G-d promises land to Abraham & descendants .... 2080/1671 B.C.E.
Abraham and Sarah 2080/1671
Egyptian slavery begins 2332/1428
Exodus from Egypt; Torah given at Mt. Sinai.......... 2448/1312
Jewish People enter Israel......................... 2488/1272
David becomes king; establishes capital in Hebron....... 2882/876
First Temple built in Jerusalem; King Solomon 2935/825
Kingdom splits into north-Israel and south-Judah 2964/769
First Temple destroyed; Babylonian exile begins 3338/423
King Cyrus allows Jews to return to Israel.............. 3391/370
Purim events in Persia 3405/355
Second Temple built in Jerusalem 3408/352
Alexander the Great and Greeks arrive in Israel 3448/312
Hasmonean-Maccabee revolt; Chanukah 3597/165
Second Temple destroyed; Roman exile begins......... 3830/70 C.E.
Rabbi Akiva is Israel's leading sage 3840/80
Bar Kochba leads failed revolt against Rome............. 3853/93
Mishna completed in Beit Shearim 3979/219
Harsh Byzantine rule begins under Constantine......... 4072/312
Jerusalem Talmud compiled in Tiberias 4128/368
Muslims conquer Jerusalem; rule from Damascus........ 4398/638
Al Aksa mosque built on Temple Mount 4420/660
Dome of the Rock built on Temple Mount.............. 4451/691
Abbasid Muslims rule from Baghdad.................. 4510/750
Christian crusaders conquer Jerusalem................ 4859/1099
Maimonides buried in Tiberias 4964/1204
Arrival of 300 French families 4971/1211
Egyptian Mamelukes conquer the region.............. 5051/1291
Jews expelled from Spain settle in Safed.............. 5243/1493

*The next five hundred years of Jewish history in Israel
can be found on page 94.*

always Home

2

Leaving It All Behind

Sarah Sonnenfeld was a passionately idealistic young woman whose husband, Rabbi Chaim Sonnenfeld, seemed destined for a position of rabbinical leadership in Hungary. In 1873, though, this idealistic couple decided to move to the land of Israel. Sarah kissed her tearful mother good-bye, left everything she knew behind, and set out for an uncertain future in the holy city of Jerusalem.

In the decades before World War I, Rabbi Abraham Shaag stood out as an outstanding rabbinical leader of European Jewry. The Hungarian Jewish community frequently looked to him to represent their interests in the courts of kings and noblemen. In 1868, unbeknownst to his community, Rabbi Shaag asked his son, a successful businessman, to move his family to the land of Israel, and make preparations for the rest of the family to follow.

When Rabbi Shaag and his family eventually boarded a ship headed for Jaffa—the port city in the Ottoman territory of Palestine—they were accompanied by Chaim and Sarah Sonnenfeld. It was the spring of 1873, and they were all going home.

The stories of the Shaag and Sonnenfeld families are but two of thousands that took place over the centuries. Though Sarah

Sonnenfeld's husband, Rabbi Chaim Sonnenfeld, went on to become the chief rabbi of Jerusalem, the names and life stories of the vast majority of those who emigrated have long been forgotten. At the same time, a survey of those we do know who emigrated over the last thousand years reveals a veritable who's who of people who made lasting contributions to the life of the Jewish people.

We will soon meet some of the most influential Jews of the last millennia who chose to make the land of Israel their home. First, however, we will touch on what remained of Jewish life in Israel after the destruction of the Second Temple.

From Rome to Holy Rome

On the ninth day of the Hebrew month of Av, in the year 70 C.E., Roman troops under the leadership of Titus crushed the defenders of Jerusalem. That same day, the Second Temple went up in flames. Since then, the Ninth of Av has been observed as a day of fasting and bitter mourning.

Though an independent Jewish state became a thing of the past, the next three hundred years were still fruitful ones for the Jewish people in the land of Israel. Even in the aftermath of widespread massacres at the hands of the Romans, a large Jewish presence still remained in the country, particularly in the Galilee. Israel at the time was a well-cultivated land, and the majority of the Jews lived in farming villages of a few thousand people. The economy was centered on a flourishing oil and wine industry, and major academies of study in places like Yavneh, Tiberias, Beit Shearim, and Cesarea, took the place of fallen Jerusalem. Though greatly reduced in number, the Jewish community in Israel still occupied a vibrant place in the life of the Jewish people.

In about the year 200 C.E., a text, whose significance remains unparalleled, was completed under the auspices of Rabbi Yehuda HaNasi (Judah the Prince) in the town of Beit Shearim. That text is known as the *Mishnah*, and became the basis for both the Jerusalem Talmud and the Babylonian Talmud.

At the time of the completion of the Jerusalem Talmud, Jews still formed the majority of the population in Israel, but matters were about to take a sudden turn for the worse. In the year 312, the Roman general Constantine dropped paganism for Christianity in a religious conversion that changed the world and paved the way for Christian rule in the land of Israel. For the next three hundred years the Jews of Israel suffered from almost endless persecution, Jerusalem was transformed into a center of Christianity, and Jews were barred from entering the city. Eventually, the Jewish population of Israel fell to no more than five thousand.

For the next fifteen centuries, while a small number of Jews remained in Israel, it remained largely a place of dreams for most of the Jews scattered throughout the world. Nonetheless, there were always Jews for whom the dream was not enough, and who were prepared to risk everything to journey and settle in Israel.

Before Airlines Offered Kosher Meals

Before the founding of Israel's El Al Airlines, Jews who wanted to go to the Promised Land had a variety of other travel options. They could take a ship, hitch a ride on a wagon, hail a camel driver, or walk.

> *"Even the darkest periods saw a trickle of immigrants. Their letters unfold for family, spellbinding descriptions of experiences en route, by land or by sea, giving full weight, of course, to the initial encounter with the Land of Israel. Potential immigrants to Israel had a choice of several routes— by sea, from Italian shores; by land from Europe via Turkey or Syria; or they could journey over the Atlas mountains to Egypt and continue by sea, or join a caravan through the Sinai Peninsula."*
>
> Abraham David, *To Come to the Land*

Beyond the tribulations related to modes of transportation, travelers faced other trials as well. The world was a dangerous place in which to travel and doubly so for Jews. Traveling in Christian lands, Jews were often vulnerable to assault, robbery, and abuse. And, to make matters worse, there wasn't even one decent kosher restaurant along any of the routes to Israel.

Let's Make Aliyah: A Who's Who in Jewish History

On July 15, 1099, the noble knights of the Crusades entered Jerusalem and hacked to death all of its 30,000 residents, including five hundred Jews. The Crusader massacre brought two thousand years of

Jewish residence in Jerusalem to an end. Seventy years later, Rabbi Benjamin of Tudela, Spain recorded in his travel journal that there remained perhaps three thousand Jews throughout the country, with the majority living in Tiberias, Ashkelon, and Akko. The centuries that followed the Crusades were exceptionally difficult ones for Jews in Israel. Nonetheless, there was always a brave community that would never leave, and other brave Jews came to join them.

Of the thousands of Jews who made their way to the land of Israel following the Crusades, many were among the most influential scholars and leaders of the last thousand years. The following list represents just a small sampling:

Yehuda Ha-Levi (1080-1145)—physician and poet, best known as the author of the *Kuzari,* a classic of Jewish philosophy.

Rabbi Shimshon of Sens and the three hundred scholars (c. 1150-1214)—In 1211, Rabbi Shimshon led a group of three hundred French scholars and their families to Israel, and they eventually settled in the coastal town of Akko. Over the ensuing decades, many French Jews decided to join this community.

The Ramban, Nachmanides (Rabbi Moshe ben Nachman) (1194-1270)—Nachmanides was the leading sage of his day, and in 1263 he was forced to flee Spain. Four years later, the elderly sage arrived in Jerusalem. Nachmanides helped found a new synagogue in Jerusalem that remained in use until 1588. Today, the restored Ramban Synagogue is once again a thriving part of community life in the Jewish Quarter of the Old City.

Rabbi Ovadiah Yarei of Bartinora (c.1440-1515)—author of one of the most important commentaries on the Mishna, he became a leading rabbinical figure in Jerusalem in the fifteenth century.

Rabbi Yosef Karo (1488-1575)—author of the *Shulchan Aruch* (the Code of Jewish Law, the preeminent text for the laws of Jewish observance and jurisprudence), he settled in Safed after fleeing Spain and Portugal.

Rabbi Chaim Attar, the Ohr HaChaim (1696-1742)—one of Morocco's outstanding rabbinical figures, his commentary to the Torah is reckoned as indispensable. In 1742, together with his family and a group of students, Rabbi Attar moved to Israel.

Rabbi Yehudah HaChassid—In 1699, Rabbi Yehudah inspired a thousand Polish Jews to emigrate to Israel. The Yehudah HaChassid synagogue played a central part in the life of Jerusalem until it was destroyed by the Jordanians in 1948.

Kabbalah and the City of Safed

In 1492, the same Ferdinand and Isabella who sent Columbus to America, sent the Jews of Spain packing. Eventually, many Jewish families and some of Spain's leading scholars settled in Israel.

Before the expulsion, there were about three hundred Jewish families living in Safed; a century later there were over nine hundred families. Jews came in droves to Safed, from North Africa, Egypt, Turkey, Syria, Hungary and Jerusalem.

A few miles outside of Safed is Meron, the burial place of Rabbi Shimon Bar Yochai. Rabbi Shimon, a renowned talmudical period sage, was the author of the Zohar, the seminal text of mystical Kabbalah, and Safed became home to many kabbalistic all-stars in the 1500s.

Inspired Disciples

Rabbi Israel Baal Shem Tov, founder of the Chassidic movement, and Rabbi Eliyahu of Vilna, known as the Vilna Gaon, were the two most influential Jewish leaders of the eighteenth century, and each inspired hundreds of disciples to settle in the land of Israel.

At the same time that the American Revolution and the French revolution were poised to alter the course of world history, the Vilna Gaon envisioned another revolution—this one involving the reestablishment of the Jewish people in the land of Israel. The Gaon's vision included the emigration of large numbers of Jews to Israel, the settling and farming of the land in accordance with the agricultural precepts of the Torah, and the establishment of Jerusalem as the world center of Jewish study and scholarship. The Vilna Gaon himself twice tried to emigrate to Israel, but both times sickness and extreme hardship forced his return to Lithuania. The first group of seventy of the followers emigrated in 1809. From 1809 until the late 1830s, one to two hundred people a year followed in their footsteps and made the move from Europe to the land of Jewish destiny.

At the same time, many Chassidic followers of the Baal Shem Tov were also making the move to Israel. In 1777, Rabbi Menachem Mendel of Vitebsk led a group of three hundred Chassidim from Russia to Israel. Over the ensuing decades other small groups of Chassidim also settled in Israel, mostly in Safed and Tiberias. The first major Chassidic leader, Rabbi Moshe Biderman—known as the Lelover Rebbe—moved to Israel in 1850, and by 1948 many of the great Chassidic communities had established thriving communities in Israel.

Hebron: From Abraham to Slabodka

Hebron is considered one of Israel's "four holy cities." The others are Safed, Tiberias, and of course, Jerusalem. Abraham and Sarah are buried together in Hebron, as are all the other patriarchs and matriarchs of the Jewish people, with the exception of Rachel, who is buried in Bethlehem.

The small Jewish community in Hebron began to grow in the 1500s, and in the early twentieth century Hebron was an important part of the Jewish return to the land of Israel. In 1924, Rabbis Nossan Tzvi Finkel and Moshe Mordecai Epstein emigrated with over a hundred of their students to Hebron where they established a branch of the famed Slabodka yeshiva. In 1929, an Arab pogrom broke out in the city. Fifty-nine men, women, and children were slaughtered, including twenty-four yeshiva students. Hundreds were injured, and virtually every Jewish home was looted; the survivors were evacuated to Jerusalem. This massacre marked the end of the Jewish community in Hebron until after 1967.

One of the survivors of the Hebron massacre was a five-year-old girl named Sarah Hamburger. She died on January 22, 2002 at the age of seventy-nine, when an Arab terrorist gunned her down on the streets of Jerusalem.

No Backs to Jerusalem

For five years I lived just a few minutes' walk from the Western Wall and the Temple Mount. Early each morning, I would hear the lyrical call to prayer that was broadcast from a large speaker in the Al-Aksa mosque. The voice of the Muslim cleric calling the faithful to prayer had a haunting and enchanting sound.

Throughout the world, five times a day, Muslims take out their prayer rugs, face Mecca, and prostrate themselves in devotion to God. Even on the Temple Mount itself, when a Muslim prays, he turns his back on the Al-Aksa mosque and faces Mecca.

For a Jew, it's always been just the opposite. Our synagogues are built to face Jerusalem and when we pray it's always toward Jerusalem. The same is true in Israel—Jews always turn toward Jerusalem in prayer. And in Jerusalem itself, Jews turn to face the Temple Mount.

Throughout history—in our prayers, thoughts, and dreams—Jews have always looked to Jerusalem. For many Jews over the centuries, "Next Year in Jerusalem" was more than a prayer, a meditation, or a dream; it has been our deepest aspiration. The Jewish people never turned its back on Jerusalem, because the land of Israel and Jerusalem were home, always home.

ghetto, Napoleon, *Herzl*

3

Oh No, Not More History

The Uru Eu Wau Wau live in such a remote corner of the Amazon rainforest that they are still waiting to find out who won the American Civil War. The Chinese once built a wall twenty-five feet high, twelve feet deep, and twenty-five hundred miles long (the distance from Boston to Spokane) to keep the world out, and to a degree, it actually worked. As for the Jews, they had no such luck. The Jewish people and the land of Israel have never had the luxury of living in a historical vacuum.

In order to appreciate the return of the Jewish people to the land of Israel, and the birth of the modern State of Israel, we will need a bit of historical perspective in terms of what was going on in the world, and how major movements and events contributed to the Jewish people's turning their focus, for the first time in nineteen hundred years, to the prospect of actually going home.

Yesterday There Were No Countries

When we look at a map of the world, we see that it is neatly divided by clear black lines that indicate the borders of about two hundred countries. The world seems like a tidy place, but it wasn't always so. In fact, up until a hundred years ago almost none of the countries that we find on our maps today existed in the form that they do today.

Actually, up until a few hundred years ago even the *idea* of countries didn't exist. Only a few hundred years ago, ideas like self-determination, the natural rights of people to direct their own affairs, the fundamental equality of all human beings, and the wrongfulness of one country trying to conquer, exploit, or rule another country were revolutionary.

We will now take a brief look at an era that gave rise to both the United States and the French Revolution and see how the ideas and political developments of the time eventually led to a man named Theodor Herzl, an idea called Zionism, and the birth of the modern State of Israel.

Colonialism and Enlightenment

In the fifteenth and sixteenth centuries, a full-blown sailing craze swept across Europe. This was a time when an Italian named Columbus was discovering America and when Vasco da Gama was sailing around Africa to India. Later, while Europeans were still sailing everywhere, the Industrial Revolution created the need for natural resources on a whole new scale. This need for resources, coupled with a mastery of the seas and the seemingly natural desire for power and prestige, fueled a period of vast European colonial expansion. By the early 1800s, European powers like France, Spain, and England had discovered, subdued, and colonized vast areas of the world's acreage and half its population.

While colonialism spread European power and influence across the globe, another development, the Enlightenment, was taking root in Europe that would eventually spell the end of colonialism. The Enlightenment was an intellectual revolution that challenged the way of thinking that was at the heart of the feudal system that dominated Europe. The ideas of the Enlightenment, and the emergence of nationalism as an outgrowth of the Enlightenment, would eventually conquer both feudalism and colonialism.

For the Jews of Europe, the Enlightenment would have a twofold effect. At first, it would help pave the way for the entry of the Jew into mainstream society. Eventually, when society proved to be less Jew-friendly than had been hoped for, the idea of nationalism would give tangible expression to the age-old Jewish longing for a return to the land of Israel.

Enlightenment, Nationalism, and the Jews

For over a thousand years before the 1700s, Europeans were harnessed by religion to the church and by necessity to a feudal system of elite landowners, and monarchs to whom they were duty-bound in near animal-like servitude. Prior to the Enlightenment, the vast majority of Europeans were malnourished, illiterate pawns who could do little more than eke out the barest existence on land they worked but could never own. Power, wealth, and control lay only in the hands of the few.

The Enlightenment posited an entirely different picture of how life could look for the masses of Europe. The concept of nationalism, spawned by the Enlightenment, became a powerful force that would eventually sweep not only the American colonies and Europe but also much of the world. Enlightened nationalism advocated human liberty and the rights of the individual, and opposed the oppressive forces of the church and the monarchies and the imposition of foreign rule.

The American Revolution of 1776 and the French Revolution of 1789 were both manifestations of Enlightenment ideas. It was the French Revolution, though, and its motto of "Liberty, Equality, Fraternity," that would have a far-reaching impact on Jews and ultimately on the movement of Jews back to Israel. It was Napoleon Bonaparte, emperor of the post-revolutionary French Republic, who set into motion a process that would culminate in a specifically Jewish expression of nationalism.

Napoleon Opens the Country Club Doors

The French Revolution produced an extraordinary document called the *Declaration of the Rights of Man and of the Citizen.* The Declaration included statements such as—

Article 1. Men are born and remain free and equal in rights.

Article 6. All citizens, being equal in the eyes of the law, are equally eligible to all dignities and to all public positions and occupations...

Article 11. The free communication of ideas and opinions is one of the most precious rights of man. Every citizen may accordingly speak, write, and print with freedom...

These were truly revolutionary ideas, and if it wasn't for the fact that they didn't apply to Protestants, actors, and Jews, they would have been even more revolutionary. Eventually, in the case of the Jews, Napoleon would make a dramatic gesture toward fully including the Jews as Frenchmen within the French Republic. Here's what happened:

After becoming Emperor, Napoleon proposed that an assembly of 112 leading Jews be called to Paris where they would be presented with a list of questions. The Jews' response to those questions would determine whether or not they would be granted full entry into the citizenry of France; it was an offer they couldn't refuse. The fateful gathering took place at a grand hotel in Paris on July 29, 1806. Some of the questions presented by the emperor's personal representative that day were—

1. Can Jews and Christians marry?
2. In the eyes of the Jews, are the French considered brothers or strangers?
3. Do Jews born in France consider France to be their country? Are they willing to defend it and obey its laws?

Less than a month after the assembly, the Jewish reply assured the emperor that Jews considered themselves to be Frenchmen in every sense of the word. Even on the question of intermarriage, they were able to finesse an answer that excluded French Christians from the Biblical prohibition, by asserting that that prohibition referred to heathens of an earlier age, and surely such a status could not apply to the enlightened Christians of France.

Pleased with the Jews' response, Napoleon decided to go one step further and absolutely stunned the Jews with his next proposal. Napoleon's idea was that the ancient supreme court of Judaism, the Sanhedrin, which had once presided in Jerusalem, should be reinstated in France. By Napoleon's decree, a newly fashioned Sanhedrin met in Paris in February of 1807, where it issued the following statement: *"We no longer form a nation within a nation. France is our country. Jews, such today is your status: your obligations are outlined, your happiness is waiting."*

In essence, Napoleon had offered the Jews a carrot while holding the specter of the stick behind his back. The carrot was an invitation to a whole new era that would include the destruction of the ghetto walls, the welcoming of Jews into the trades and professions, and the opening of doors to the halls of higher education. The stick was all that the Jews had known from time immemorial—isolation, ostracism, and violent anti-Semitism.

Gorgeous Invitation, Sorry We Can't All Attend

Though the members of the Sanhedrin could not foresee the full implications of their statement, it proved to be a turning point in Jewish history. This was the end of the idea of Jewish nationhood and the beginning of Judaism as just a religion. This was the moment when Jews ceased to be members of the Jewish people and instead became Frenchmen of the Jewish faith. This radical reorientation of basic Jewish identity would express itself again and again—not only in France but also in England and elsewhere—in Reform Judaism's theological positions, in Jews' carrying the banner of socialism, and in the German Jews' tragic embrace of the Fatherland.

At the same time, large numbers of Jews looked on in horror at this shearing away of Jewish peoplehood from the rubric of Jewish identity. Many of the major rabbinical leaders of the time saw Napoleon's invitation to have a seat at the enlightened table of humanity as a kind of spiritual Trojan horse that would wreak havoc on the meaning and mission of the Jews as a unique and distinct people.

In the decades that followed, at least in Western Europe, Jews became both culturally and economically upwardly mobile on a scale that had previously seemed impossible. The story in Eastern Europe, however, was different. Napoleon's imperial designs ran aground in Russia, and thus the benefits realized by the Jews in the West were barely felt in the East.

Jewish Nationalism: All Dressed Up and Nowhere to Go

Nationalism was one of the most powerful forces unleashed by the Enlightenment and soon included the embrace of ethnic identity. For the Jews of Europe, a particularly Jewish strain of nationalism possessed an almost magical draw. Jewish nationalism led to a new interest in Jewish literature and Jewish history, and to a revival of Hebrew as a spoken language. For numerous European Jews, it became a matter of pride that they could converse and correspond in Hebrew. In the midst of a late-nineteenth-century European society that was asserting cultural pride and ethnic identity, Jewish nationalism allowed the Jew to do the same. All it lacked was a homeland to call its own.

Beneath the surface of European society lurked another force that buttressed the rise of Jewish nationalism. In Poland and Russia Jew-hatred was an open, overt force. However, even in Western Europe, no matter how enlightened and liberal Europeans became, it seemed that Jew-hatred always lay in wait. Both of these impulses—nationalism as a romantic reawakening of ancient Jewish spirit, and nationalism as a pragmatic search for self-determination in the face of anti-Semitism—would eventually find their full expression in Zionism.

In many ways, nationalism struck a natural chord with the Jews of Europe. For millennia, though most Jews were unable to actually reside in Israel, in spirit they lived there nonetheless. When Jews prayed for rain, it was the rains of Israel they prayed for. When they marked the beginning of each new month, it was according to the appearance of the new moon in Jerusalem, not in Cracow, Frankfurt, or St. Petersburg. And whether it was under the wedding canopy, on Yom Kippur, or at the Passover Seder, Jews always lived with "Next Year in Jerusalem" in their hearts and minds.

As the 1800s were coming to a close, the land of Israel (or Palestine as it was then referred to) was a place that was intensely familiar to Jewish hearts everywhere, a place that was home not only to ancient Jews and scholars but also to a contemporary community of devout Jewish families and great rabbinical leaders, and was becoming the focus of a new nationalist wave of inspiration. It was also a place that seemed to be little more than an afterthought to its Ottoman Turk overlords. Perhaps, just perhaps, the time was ripe for the Jewish people to finally turn their backs on the exile and go home.

In 1882, the ferment of Jewish nationalism coalesced in two Russian groups that called themselves *Chovavei Tzion*, "Lovers of Zion," and BILU, an acronym for "House of Jacob let us go forth." It was then that seven thousand *Chovavei Tzion* members set out to establish some of the earliest agricultural settlements in what would become in less than fifty years the modern State of Israel. Over the next eighteen years, another thirteen thousand Jews followed these lovers of Zion to Zion.

While the aims and efforts of those like the *Chovavei Tzion* were ambitious, in terms of the whole of European Jewry their numbers were still quite modest. In Russia and eastern Europe, where Jews were victimized by pogroms, the overriding desire behind most Jewish emigration was just to get out. For those who were able to get out,

America and the West seemed to be the easiest and safest havens of refuge. The land of Israel, on the other hand, while it represented a dream come true, was still largely a desolate, neglected, and dangerous backwater in the Ottoman Empire. Nonetheless, just over the horizon lay an event—and one man's response—that would spark a full-fledged and viable movement of Jews to return to their long lost home. The event was the Dreyfus Affair in France, the man was an assimilated Viennese Jewish journalist named Theodor Herzl, and the movement would be called Zionism.

From "the Affair" in France...

The Dreyfus Affair was as big in France as the O.J. trial was in the United States, and it dragged on for even longer. Here's what happened:

In September of 1894, French counterintelligence discovered irrefutable evidence that one of its own was passing valuable information to the Germans. The question was, "Whodunnit?" At the time, a Jew by the name of Alfred Dreyfus was working in military intelligence, and, despite the fact that Jews had been accepted in French society for almost a century, there was no shortage of Frenchman who wished those ghetto walls had never come down—so they decided to get Dreyfus. Soon, "secret" evidence pointing directly to Dreyfus was uncovered. The accusations against Dreyfus the Jew were trumpeted in the unabashedly anti-Semitic French press, and news of a Jewish traitor was well received—and loudly echoed—by Catholic leaders and laity alike. In short order, Dreyfus was convicted, court-martialed, and sent to rot in a filthy, vermin-infested cell on Devil's Island off the coast of French Guiana.

While Alfred Dreyfus was rotting away in prison, a re-examination of the evidence clearly pointed to another man and pressure for a retrial began to mount. The whole "affair," as it became known, was the political event of the day across Europe. Eventually the officer who was behind the phony evidence killed himself, and though Dreyfus was once again found to be guilty, this time French President Emile Loubet pardoned him before he began to serve his sentence—which brings us to Theodor Herzl.

...To the Basel in Switzerland

Theodor Herzl was a writer, a liberal idealist, and a journalist. As a man, he was someone who believed deeply in the ideas of the Enlightenment, and in France and Germany as beacons for Europe and the world. Herzl was well-educated, urbane, and a captivating speaker. Born in Hungary, he was raised in Austria by wealthy and influential parents who identified deeply with German nationalism and with its culture and ideals. Though his parents retained their Jewish identity, the Herzls lived in a time when it was common for Jews to be baptized and formally opt out of their identity. Ironically, though Judaism was just a footnote to Herzl's life, it would be his vision of the Jewish future that would have as dramatic and enduring an impact on the next century as anyone else's.

As a journalist, Herzl covered a number of political rallies where anti-Semitism was openly expressed, but none of these prepared him for the shock of "the affair." Herzl was a foreign correspondent from Vienna covering the Dreyfus trial in Paris, and was deeply affected by the outpouring of Jew-hatred that spewed forth from the capital of enlightened Europe. This experience convinced Herzl that anti-Semitism was a condition that could never be remedied in Europe.

After the Dreyfus Affair, Herzl became obsessed with finding a cure for anti-Semitism. The cure he found was in the idea of a Jewish homeland. To Herzl, because the Jewish people had no state of their own, they were doomed to always being outsiders in history, and as outsiders they would always be held in contempt and despised. But a Jewish state could rectify this, and so by 1896 Herzl had written a small book that contained his prescription for anti-Semitism. It was entitled, *The Jewish State*, and it argued that the creation of a Jewish state would eliminate the fundamental difference between the Jews and all other people, and thus eradicate the cause of anti-Semitism.

Ironically, though Herzl became totally devoted to the idea of a Jewish homeland, he was so alienated from Judaism that it never occurred to him that his idea would strike a profoundly deep chord within the Jewish people. In fact, because of his paucity of Jewish sensibilities, Herzl was at times willing to consider both Argentina and Uganda as possible sites for the Jewish homeland. As Judaism was an afterthought in his life, so originally were Jerusalem and the land of Israel afterthoughts to his concept of a Jewish state.

To be sure, Herzl was derided from many sides, but clearly, he couldn't be accused of lacking determination. With time, Herzl became utterly determined to create an organized movement of the Jewish masses capable of building a homeland that would include everything one could find in any other country. Eventually, he became equally determined that the place for this homeland must be in Palestine.

On August 29, 1897, Theodor Herzl convened the first Zionist Congress in Basel, Switzerland. The Congress was attended by 204 delegates from across Europe (though almost half were from Russia) and spanned the spectrum of Jewish identity, association, and affiliation. In Basel, a flag for the Jewish homeland was unfurled, "Hatikva" was sung as the Jewish national anthem, and it became clear that the Jews were abundantly serious about where they were headed—to what then was Ottoman-ruled Palestine and what today is the State of Israel. In his diary, Herzl wrote, "In Basel, I created the Jewish state."

Next Year in Jerusalem

Less than a year after the first Zionist Congress, over a thousand Zionist societies had been established across Europe, predominantly in Russia, and even some in America. The living dream of "Next Year in Jerusalem," combined with Herzl's uncanny idea of establishing a Jewish state and the desperate need of Russia's Jews to escape the stranglehold of the Czar, all combined to fuel a movement—the Zionist movement—that would alter the course of Jewish history. After two thousand years, the Jews, not just as individuals or families, but as a people, were ready to go home.

The obstacles along the road from Basel to Jerusalem were remarkably daunting. Palestine was still ruled by the same Ottoman Empire that had conquered it almost four hundred years earlier. World War I—a war that would devastate Europe and throw European Jewry into a pit of chaos and upheaval—was yet to be waged. Palestine would still have to pass from the hands of the Turks to the hands of the British. World War II, and the destruction of seven out of every ten Jews in Europe, was still a distant catastrophe, and the newly established Arab states of the Middle East would yet try to crush the Jews and their Jewish home. Eventually, however, Israel would be reborn.

Zionism the Vortex

While Zionism was a remarkable idea, and a history-altering movement, not all Jews embraced it. Zionism became an ideological vortex that no Jew could escape. Whether you loved it, rejected it, or fought to redefine it, Jews everywhere couldn't help but confront it and be confronted by it. The following list of ideological responses is not comprehensive. Its purpose is just to provide a sense of how various elements within the Jewish people have dealt with Zionism.

Herzl's National-Political Zionists:

These were bottom-line pragmatists and they had a plan. Step by step, they were prepared to put the political and economic pieces in place that would provide the basis for the infrastructure of a modern state capable of absorbing immigrants and moving them into the endeavors needed to build a viable political entity. People like Chaim Weizmann exemplified their commitment to working within Europe's existing political structure to bring about the realization of Herzl's vision. Weizmann was able to use his connections, prestige, and eloquence to advance the cause of a Jewish homeland at the highest levels of government. He would eventually become the first president of Israel.

Achad Ha'am's Cultural Zionists:

This was Zionism with a soul. Achad Ha'am (born Asher Ginsberg) held in disdain a Zionist vision that stripped the Jewish people of a spiritual core. To Achad Ha'am, Herzl's idea of a Jewish state was little more than a kind of assimilation writ large, and he told Herzl as much. To the Cultural Zionists, for a state that happened to be populated by Jews to in fact be a *Jewish* state, it would have to also become the cultural and spiritual center of the Jewish people.

Reform Non-Zionists:

Leopold Stein, a prominent leader of Reform Jewry in Germany, wrote, "We know but one fatherland, that in which we live. We cannot pray as though our present home were strange to us and our true home lay a thousand miles distant." This statement was echoed in America in 1897 when the reform movement's Central Conference of American Rabbis formally condemned political Zionism. It was only much later, when it became obvious that Germany represented the end of Jewish life—and not a golden future—that Reform leaders like Rabbi Abba Hillel Silver so ably took up the cause of a Jewish homeland in Palestine.

Socialist Zionists:

In Russia, Jews were playing a central role in advancing the wave of socialism that would do away with czarist Russia and its centuries of oppression, and replace it with the imagined utopia of communism. In the main, these Jews were opposed to Zionism both ideologically and because it in no way addressed the reality of millions of Jews who in all likelihood would remain on Russian and European soil. Eventually, a young intellectual named Ber Borochov proposed a theory of Marxist Zionism that envisioned a Jewish state built on the principles of Engels and Marx. This was the beginning of Labor Zionism, and most of the thirty thousand Russian Jews who immigrated to Palestine between 1905 and 1914 came with this ideology in mind. Many of Israel's founders, builders and political leaders—people like David Ben-Gurion, Moshe Dayan and Yitzchak Rabin—were Labor Zionists, and it was Labor Zionism that would place a far-reaching socialist stamp on economic and social policy during Israel's formative period.

Religious Zionists:

A number of prominent rabbinical figures, including Rabbi Naftali Tzvi Yehuda Berlin, Rabbi Meir Leibush Malbim, and most notably, Rabbi Tzvi Hirsch Kalischer contributed their scholarly perspectives on the significance of the land of Israel to the movement that would become the *Chovavei Tzion*, the Lovers of Zion. In 1893, Rabbi Shmuel Mohliver founded *mercaz ruchani*, the "spiritual center" that would later, under Rabbi Yitzchak Yaacov Reines, become the Mizrachi party.

Religious Zionism saw the return to the land as a spiritually natural extension of all that Judaism represented and viewed any break with traditional Torah-based Judaism as an abandonment of that which had brought the Jews to the verge of return in the first place. Religious Zionism sought to work from within the general Zionist movement and Rabbi Avraham Yitchak Kook, the first chief rabbi of Palestine, became a powerful advocate for the inclusion of Zionism in the rubric of a Torah-true outlook on Judaism, Jewish history, and Jewish destiny.

Religious Non-Zionists:

In order to make sure that their voice was heard in the Jewish world and beyond, and in order to counter the trend of abandoning Judaism that was present in the Zionist movement, 204 of Jewry's most distinguished rabbis gathered in 1912 for the founding of *Agudas Israel*. These were the *chareidim*, those who today are referred to as the ultra-orthodox. For centuries, these were the people who risked everything to settle in the land of Israel. Ironically, it was these same people who rejected Zionism.

To the political Zionist, the future and well-being of the Jewish people was dependent on the creation and well-being of a Jewish state. To the religious non-Zionist, just the opposite was true. The well-being of a Jewish state was dependent on the well-being of the Jewish people, and the well-being of the Jewish people was dependent on its ability to fulfill its calling as defined by the teachings and practices of the Torah. Amongst these non-Zionists, there was a minority that rejected any form of pre-messianic Jewish sovereignty.

Bagels & Lox Zionists

These were the Jews who weren't all that interested in Zionist ideology and who were never going to settle in Israel but who nonetheless believed with all their hearts that it was critical for the Jews to have a country of their own. In the wake of World War II, these were the masses of Jews in the United States and elsewhere whose unflagging support for the Jewish state expressed itself in financial support, political activism, and countless visits to Israel that made them feel so proud to be Jews.

Israel, Here We Come

On the day that Herzl convened the first Zionist Congress in 1897, there were about 60,000 Jews living in Ottoman Palestine. Forty years later, there were nearly half-a-million Jews living in British Palestine, and twenty years after that, there were almost two million Jews living in Israel, including 600,000 who had been expelled from Arab countries after the birth of the Jewish state.

That the Jewish people kept the dream of a return to Zion alive for over two thousand years is a remarkable phenomenon. That this dream manifested itself in the re-establishment of a Jewish state after twenty-five centuries is an event utterly unique in the annals of human history.

the disputed
Land

II

Balfour, Ben-Gurion, and too *much War*

4

Wasteland Israel

The land of Israel was once part of a great fertile region that produced an abundance of agriculture; and then came destruction. From the time of the Roman conquest, Palestine had been ruled by outsiders who had little interest in the well-being and productivity of the land. The Muslims conquered the land in 638 and never seriously developed the country. Later, wars between the Christian crusaders and the Muslims created a virtual wasteland. The Mongol invaders who arrived in 1260 destroyed many of the villages in Palestine. The Mamelukes who followed them burned and sacked towns and villages, uprooted orchards, and filled drinking wells. A vastly productive agricultural region had been reduced to swamps ruled by malaria-infested mosquitoes. In 1351, the Black Death ravaged Palestine, and by 1500 its entire population declined to barely 200,000 people. Imagine Pennsylvania with only 200,000 people. Palestine was *empty*. As the winter of 1516 approached, Jerusalem was an impoverished city whose once mighty walls were a distant memory and whose residents were at the mercy of disease and Bedouin raiders.

On December 1, 1516, the Turkish sultan Selim I and his army advanced on a defenseless Jerusalem. The Ottoman Empire had arrived. The Jewish population of Israel at the time was approximately 3,000, with the majority living in Safed, and only six to eight hundred of the most devoted Jews clinging to precious, poverty-stricken Jerusalem. A later sultan, Suleiman the Magnificent, took a great interest in Jerusalem, had its walls fully restored for the first time in centuries, and built large pools to provide water for the city. The majestic walls and gates of Suleiman still encircle the Old City of Jerusalem. By 1550, thanks to improved living conditions and Turkish control of the Bedouins, the Jewish population of Jerusalem rose to over 1,000 people, and in Safed to approximately 5,000.

Ultimately, though, Suleiman's intense interest in Jerusalem proved to be an anomaly, with the prevailing Turkish attitude being largely one of indifference. For the most part, its primary interest was in the revenues that could be extracted from taxes levied on farmers and fees paid by pilgrims who made their way to Jerusalem. By the early 1800s, the Ottoman Empire itself was well on its way to decline, the economic situation in Palestine was in shambles, and Bedouin robbers again had free reign to terrorize the population. At the turn of the nineteenth century, there were about 6,000 Jews living in Palestine. The squalor and deplorable hygienic conditions that had returned to Jerusalem made it all but uninhabitable. It was only thanks to the beginnings of British influence in the region that conditions began to improve to the point that the Jewish population grew to 17,000 by 1850.

As the nineteenth century was drawing to a close, the arrival of the British in the Middle East, the imminent collapse of the Ottoman Empire, anti-Semitism in Europe, and the stirrings of modern Zionism would all converge to pave the way for a new Middle East and the rejuvenation of the Jewish people in the land of Israel.

We're Back

Between 1882 and 1903, 25,000 Jews moved from Europe to Palestine. These immigrants were motivated by a desire to reside in the Holy Land, by Zionism, and by the need to flee czarist Russia. Conditions in Palestine at the time were harsh, and not all the immigrants remained. Nonetheless, the modern return of the Jewish people to the land of Israel was underway. By 1900, some 50,000 Jews were living in Palestine. The population in Jerusalem at the turn of the century consisted of 28,000 Jews and 17,000 Muslims and Christians. The rest of the Jews lived in Jaffa, Hebron, Haifa, Tiberias and Safed, though 5,000 were living in newly established agricultural settlements. To many of the early Zionists, these agricultural settlements held the key to a large-scale return to the land of Israel. It was agricultural development that would bring the land back to life and create the industry and infrastructure that could support large-scale immigration. For many, the idea of the Jew as a farmer and reclaimer of the land also represented the transformation of the Jews from European city-dwellers into a new kind of rugged, pioneering Jew. Between 1904 and 1914, another 30,000 Jews, the majority of whom came from Russia, set out for Palestine. These 30,000 Jews, most of whom were socialists who had abandoned their religious roots, would set the tone for the early development of the Jewish presence in Palestine, and eventually for the State of Israel.

> *"Their notion of pioneering was a kind of secular messianism. They had come, too, not merely to establish a Socialist commonwealth but to rebuild their nationhood, their very manhood, by the sweat of their brows."*
>
> Howard M. Sachar, *A History of Israel*

By the first decade of the twentieth century, Baron Rothschild was financing the establishment of agricultural settlements in Palestine, a bank had been founded to help finance Jewish development, and the Jewish National Fund began to purchase land in Palestine and to support the training of agricultural workers. The Turkish government was tolerant of Jewish immigration, calculating that the Jews would bring money, investment, and development, which would help line the pockets of the empire. By 1914, there were 85,000 Jews living in Ottoman Palestine, dozens of Jewish agricultural settlements dotted the landscape, and Jews had purchased over 100,000 acres of land.

When World War I broke out at the end of 1914, the pieces were in place for the creation of a Jewish state in Palestine. The degree in which the Jews had developed Palestine in less than thirty years was unlike anything that had been seen before, and the contours of a new society were quickly taking hold.

So Who Was Balfour and What Did He Declare?

The British were fighting World War I with one eye on defeating the Turks and another on how to best position themselves in the Middle

East after the war. In the fall of 1915, Shareif Hussein of Mecca—patriarch of the Hashemite family, and Arabia's most prestigious tribal leader—secretly committed the Hashemites to aid the English against the Turks. In return, it was expected that the Hashemite family would become the anointed rulers of the vast Arabic lands that the British would take from the Turks. The Hashemites would have their power and prestige and the British would have their proxy. It seemed like a good deal; but Great Britain wasn't finished dealing. A few months later, Great Britain entered into another secret agreement, this one with France and Russia. In the Sykes-Picot-Sazanov Agreement, Russia would get Turkey, France would get Syria (including Palestine and Lebanon) and part of Mesopotamia (Iraq), while Great Britain would get Transjordan and the other part of Mesopotamia. This is where Arthur James Balfour appears on the scene.

Arthur Balfour was a prominent British politician who had a Jewish friend by the name of Chaim Weizmann. Originally from Russia, Chaim Weizmann was one of Great Britain's most highly regarded chemists, the leader of British Jewry and a devoted Zionist. At the beginning of the war, Weizmann was asked by the British government to help develop new types of explosives. His success in doing so positioned him to be able to influence people like future prime minister Lloyd George and future foreign secretary Arthur Balfour. Soon it would be time for another British deal.

As the war progressed, the British began looking for a way to undermine France's designs on Palestine, and the Jews were perfectly positioned to help out. With the British army advancing on Palestine, and with the Jews of Palestine prepared to accept some kind of autonomy under the umbrella of the British Empire, the table was set for the issuance of the Balfour Declaration. On November 2, 1917, on behalf of the British government, Foreign Secretary Balfour penned the following letter to Lord Rothschild, head of the British Zionist movement:

Dear Lord Rothschild,

I have much pleasure in conveying to you, on behalf of His Majesty's Government, the following declaration of sympathy with Jewish Zionist aspirations which had been submitted to, and approved by, the Cabinet: "His Majesty's Government views with favor the establishment in Palestine of a national home for the Jewish people, and will use their best endeavors to facilitate the achievement of this object, it being clearly understood that nothing shall be done that may prejudice the civil and religious rights of existing non-Jewish communities in Palestine, or the rights and political status enjoyed by Jews in any other country."

Jewish response to this brief letter was euphoric. People literally danced in the streets. In the blink of an eye, it seemed as if a two–thousand-year-old dream was about to come true. Six weeks later, on December 11—the second day of Chanukah—General Allenby and his British forces entered Jerusalem. The fate of Palestine was now in the hands of the British.

World War I and the New Middle East

Once upon a time, the Middle East was a difficult place to understand, and then it got totally confusing. After four centuries of Ottoman rule in the region, its hegemony was challenged by Great Britain and finally ended in World War I. Today's Middle East is rooted in the aftermath of World War I. For the sake of background and context, it will be helpful to take a look at the origins of the present-day Middle East. Here's a quick overview.

Egypt—Though formally part of the Ottoman Empire, Great Britain had controlled Egypt since 1882. In large part, Great Britain's desire to maintain a presence in Egypt was due to the Suez Canal, an enormous strategic asset. In 1919, anti-British strikes and riots swept Egypt, and in 1922 Egypt gained its independence. In 1952, Colonel Gamal Abdel Nasser came to power in a coup deposing King Farouk. Nasser was a charismatic leader whose ambition was to unite all the Arab countries. In 1967, Nasser led the charge to destroy Israel; within six days he was dealt a crushing defeat. Nasser was succeeded by Anwar Sadat, who masterminded the 1973 Yom Kippur surprise attack on Israel and later, in 1979, signed the peace accords with Menachem Begin and Jimmy Carter at Camp David.

Syria—In April 1920, France received a mandate over Syria (including what is today Lebanon). At the time, Syria was being run by Feisel Hussein, who had been installed by Great Britain as thanks for the Husseinis' help in the war. This setup proved to be problematic, because the dominant clans and factions of Syria viewed both Hussein and France as outsiders. Eventually France occupied Damascus, exiled Feisel to Iraq, and divided Syria in two, creating Syria and Lebanon. Among other things, this helps to explain why Syria has always had ambitions on Lebanon. In the Six-Day War of 1967, Israel captured the Golan Heights from Syria. In 1971, Hafez Al-Assad came to power in a coup. He was a brutal leader who once massacred over 20,000 Syrian civilians as a warning against opposition. Assad was Sadat's partner in the 1973 Yom Kippur War, though he never followed Sadat down the road to peace and remained, to his dying day, a perilous enemy of Israel.

Lebanon—In case you missed it, go back and reread what took place in Syria. By the 1960s, Beirut had become the French Riviera of the Middle East. Sadly, a civil war in 1975, Syrian intervention-turned-occupation in 1976, and the establishment of a PLO mini-state in southern Lebanon ravaged what had been the jewel of the Arab world. Israel's 1982 invasion in pursuit of the PLO only added to the decline of Lebanon.

Saudi Arabia—Arabia, the vast desert peninsula that is home to Mecca, Medina, and lots of oil, was also home to two powerful families—the Hussein family in the west and the Ibn Saud family in the east. In 1918, Sharif Hussein was driven into exile, leaving Ibn Saud at the top of the sand dunes; thus the name Saudi Arabia. In 1936, an American company discovered oil in Saudi Arabia and today Saudi Arabia is the world's largest producer of oil. In 1991, the United States and its allies fought the Gulf War against Iraq to protect the oil fields of Saudi Arabia and Kuwait. It was something of an embarrassment for Saudi Arabia to have to be rescued by infidels from the West. Worse yet would have been if the Jews had helped the allies save the Saudis; so the Saudis insisted that they would only allow America to save them if it promised that Israel wouldn't be allowed to help. Go figure.

Iraq—After World War I, Mesopotamia came under the administration of British India. The situation didn't go well for Great Britain, and the disparate tribes and clans united in revolt. Eventually, Great Britain established an Arab monarchy, placed Feisel Hussein (who had been exiled from Syria) at the helm, and by 1932 Iraq became fully independent. In 1979, Saddam Hussein came to power; that was bad. Bad for the people of Iraq, bad for the world, and bad for Israel. In response to US, British, and Saudi attacks on Iraq during the Gulf War, Saddam Hussein launched a series of scud missile attacks against Tel Aviv. Go figure.

Iran—The Persian empire was founded around 550 B.C.E. and, until 1935, what is today known as Iran was always known as Persia. Persia long ago became the center of Shiite Islam, and Iran remains so today. The Shiites are committed to making sure that matters of state adhere to Islamic principles. In 1978, Ayatollah Khomeini led a revolution that overthrew the Shah of Iran, who was seen as leading Iran away from strict Islam and into the hands of the West in general, and the United States (a.k.a. "The Great Satan") in particular. Khomeini was responsible for the introduction of suicide killings in the name of Islam, and his first target was the US Marine barracks in Lebanon, where a suicide bomber killed hundreds. Today, Iran is a major sponsor of terrorism, and is bad news for Israel (a.k.a. "The Little Satan"). Terrorists in Lebanon, the West Bank, and Gaza, whose goal is to destroy Israel, receive major financial backing from Iran.

Jordan—In 1921, Great Britain divided Palestine along the Jordan River. The eastern side became the kingdom of Transjordan while the western portion continued to be called Palestine and remained under British rule until 1948. In 1951, King Abdullah was assassinated by a Palestinian who was outraged by the king's apparent openness to dealing amicably with the Jews of Israel. Abdullah's seventeen-year-old grandson, King Hussein, assumed the throne and reigned until his death in 2000. King Hussein was duped by his fellow Arab leaders into joining what they assured him would be a victorious war against Israel in 1967. To his dismay, Egypt and Syria were routed and in less than a week Jordan had lost the West Bank and eastern Jerusalem to Israel. In 1970, Hussein fought a war to drive the PLO out of Jordan. In 1973, he joined the attack against Israel in the Yom Kippur War and in 2000 he signed a peace treaty with Israel.

The Decisive Years

We'll now take a look at the defining events, moments, and decisions that unfolded in Palestine from the end of World War I until Israel achieved independence in 1948. These were the make-or-break years that would determine if Israel would come to be, and, if it would, how that would happen. This period would also have a seminal impact on the future conflict between Israel and the Arab nations, as well as the Israeli-Palestinian conflict.

San Remo, Anybody?

Following the war, in April 1920, in San Remo, Italy, the British and the French were once again at the bargaining table dividing up the Middle East. This time, though France got to keep Syria, Great Britain received a mandate over Palestine. The borders of the Palestine Mandate included what is today Israel and Jordan, that is, both sides of the Jordan River. (See map on page 152). Over the course of the next year, events occurred that dramatically affected the Palestine Mandate and the whole future of the Middle East.

Without going into the details, here's what happened. France ended up dividing Syria into Syria and Lebanon, and in 1921 Great Britain divided Palestine into Transjordan and Palestine. Transjordan (later known as Jordan), occupied three-quarters of Palestine and was given to Prince Abdullah, the son of Sharif Hussein. Following the creation of Transjordan, Great Britain's commitment to a Jewish homeland would have to be realized in what was left of Palestine west of the Jordan River.

Though disappointed by the sudden truncating of Palestine, the Jews were still happy that their dream of a Jewish State might come true, if only in western Palestine. The Arabs of western Palestine, however, were less than thrilled with the prospects of a Jewish homeland at all.

From Lord Balfour to Lord Peel:
When Push Came to Shove

The Balfour Declaration and the British mandate for Palestine opened the way for implementing the creation of a reborn Jewish state. At the time there were 600,000 Arabs and 85,000 Jews living in Palestine, and 90 percent of the potentially productive land lay fallow and undeveloped. The Zionist vision at the time looked like this: over the course of the coming decades, Jewish immigration would continually increase until the Jews were a majority in Palestine. At that point, the Jews would be able to create a uniquely Jewish country. It was generally assumed that there would be a substantial Arab community in Israel, that the Arabs would become citizens of the country, and that, like the Jews, the Arabs would benefit greatly from the development of the country.

> *"The country's irrigable plains are capable of supporting a population of six million. It is on these lands that the Jewish people demands the right to establish its homeland. Both the vision of social justice and the equality of all peoples that the Jewish people has cherished for three thousand years require absolutely and unconditionally that the rights and interests of the non-Jewish inhabitants of the country be guarded and honored punctiliously."*
>
> David Ben-Gurion, written during a 1918 trip to the United States to gain support for immigration to Palestine.

From 1920 to 1921, 16,000 Jews arrived in Palestine. In the Arab community at the time, there were some who saw the potential for mutual benefit in the arrival of the Jews and others who saw the Jews and their idea of establishing a state as anathema. To the latter, World War I was just like the Crusades, only worse. The Christians were back, and this time they were bringing the Jews with them.

Some Arab voices sounded like this:

> *"The Arabs, especially the educated among us, look with deep sympathy on the Zionist movement. We will wish the Jews a hearty welcome home. Our two movements [Arab nationalism and Zionism] complete one another. The Jewish movement is nationalist and not imperialist. Our movement is nationalist and not imperialist, and there is room in Syria for both of us. Indeed, I think that neither can be a real success without the other. I look forward, and my people with me look forward, to a future in which we will help you and you will help us, so that the countries in which we are mutually interested may once again take their places in the community of civilized peoples of the world."*
>
> Emir Feisel Hussein, March 1919
> From a letter to Zionist leader Felix Frankfurter, following the emir's meetings with Chaim Weizmann in Paris.

Other Arab voices sounded like this:

"Remember that the Jew is your strong enemy, and the enemy of your ancestors. Do not be misled by his tricks, for it is he who tortured Christ and poisoned Muhammad. It is he who now endeavors to slaughter you, as he did yesterday."

From a 1920 pamphlet issued by a group
called the Jerusalem Arab Students.

This group, and other Arab nationalist groups, were guided by the teachings of Haj Amin al-Husseini.

"All the troubles started at Zurich, where the Jews held a conference in August and were assured the aid of the rich American Jews for building up Palestine. This made the Palestine Jews so arrogant that they thought they could start driving us out of our country."

Grand Mufti Haj Amin al-Husseini, 1929.
A sarcastic comment on the deadly anti-Jewish
riots that he himself had instigated.

During the war, al-Husseini met with Hitler in Berlin to solicit his help against their common enemy, the Jews. Hitler assured the Mufti that when the hour arrived Germany would assist in "the destruction of the Jewish element residing in the Arab sphere."

Unfortunately, it was the voice of Haj Amin al-Husseini and his followers that won the day. In 1921, al-Husseini, who viewed both the British and the Jews as infidels violating Muslim land, instigated deadly riots against the Jews. Arabs raided Jewish farms across the country and killed forty-seven people. After the British authorities restored calm, they took two steps in an effort to mollify the Arabs. First, they placed a temporary ban on Jewish immigration, and second, they elevated al-Husseini to the position of Grand Mufti, thus making him the supreme religious authority in Palestine. It was hoped that these moves would soothe Arab feelings; in fact, they served to whet the Arabs' appetite for further action against the Jews.

"It is not clear whether a Jewish-Arab agreement to work together in Palestine would have been feasible even under sensible Arab leadership. But it became absolutely impossible

*once Haj Amin became Grand Mufti. The Mufti was able to
infect the Pan-Arab movement with his violent anti-Zionism.
The somber achievement of the Grand Mufti was to open a
chasm between the Jewish and Arab leadership."*

Paul Johnson, *A History of the Jews*

Between 1922 and 1928, another 84,000 Jews arrived in Palestine. New Jewish farming settlements were established, Jewish industry was expanded, and Jewish shops and businesses were opened in the cities. At the same time, the voice of the Mufti persisted in stirring Arab anger and resentment. In 1929, terrible anti-Jewish riots again broke out across the country. The Jewish Quarter of Jerusalem was attacked, Jews were murdered and their homes torched in Safed, and in Hebron sixty men, women, and children were butchered, including the rabbis and students of the famed Hebron yeshiva. In the end, 133 Jews were murdered and almost 400 more were wounded—many were women and children.

In 1933, Adolph Hitler came to power in Germany. That year, Jewish immigration jumped from 12,000 the year before to 37,000. Jews from Germany, Austria, and Czechoslovakia came to Palestine in unprecedented numbers. As the skies darkened for the Jews of Europe, more and more looked to Palestine. In 1934, 45,000 Jews arrived, and in 1935—the year that the Nuremberg Laws were enacted—66,000 arrived.

By the mid-1930s, the Arabs of western Palestine were looking to independence, to putting an end to the prospect of a Jewish state, and to driving the British out of Palestine. The British, for their part, were seriously reassessing their position in Palestine, and the wisdom of the Balfour Declaration was beginning to look rather suspect.

The year 1936 proved to be the straw that broke the British back. In the spring, fresh Arab violence turned into widespread attacks on Jews and a revolt against the British. In addition to armed confrontation with the British, the Mufti called for a general strike of all Arab workers aimed at crippling the local economy. Six months after the revolt began, thousands of acres of Jewish farmland and orchards had been destroyed, 21 Jewish men, women, and children were dead, and 140 Arabs had been killed in fights with the British that left 33 British soldiers dead and many wounded.

It should be mentioned that the Jews were not completely defenseless. Though it was illegal for Jews to carry arms or organize any kind of militia, after the riots in the twenties, a clandestine self-defense organization—the Hagganah—was formed. The Hagganah made illegal arms purchases and provided secret training for Jewish men and women. Jewish casualties would have been even higher in 1936 if not for the existence of the Hagganah.

In 1936, Palestine was at a crossroads, and it would be left to a man named Lord Peel to chart its future direction. Everything was about to change.

A Simple Piece of White Paper

When the fighting ended in the fall of 1936, the British had had enough. A commission of inquiry, chaired by Lord Peel, was established to make a thorough study of the situation in Palestine. In July of 1937, the Peel Commission issued its recommendation that Palestine be partitioned into two countries, one Arab and one Jewish. Response from both communities was not long in coming. In August, the Zionist Congress voted to accept partition but with modified borders. This miniscule state about the size of Delaware was a far cry from what the Jews had envisioned twenty years earlier. Nonetheless, they were prepared to accept it. The following month, four hundred Arab delegates representing all the Arab states and Palestine met in Damascus. Their response to Lord Peel was a total rejection of partition, a rejection of the notion of a Jewish state, and the issuance of a virtual ultimatum to the British—"Choose between our friendship and that of the Jews."

The Arab rejection of partition eventually led to a more drastic British policy. In March 1939, the British issued a White Paper that declared the following: (1) Jewish immigration would be limited to a total of no more than 75,000 over the next five years, (2) it would now be illegal for any more land to be sold to Jews in Palestine, and (3) in ten years time a state would be established in Palestine under the principle of majority rule. It was anticipated that the population in Palestine would by then stand at around one million Arabs and half a million Jews.

The British had made their choice, and their interests clearly lay with the Arabs. For the Jews, what had begun with a short letter and so much hope, now seemed to be ending with yet another piece of paper.

In September of 1939, the Germans invaded Poland. World War

II was underway, and everywhere the Jewish people was faced with enemies. The British had virtually closed Palestine to the Jewish people; those Jews who were in Palestine were surrounded by hostile Arabs; and the Germans were about to begin shipping Jews to the crematoria of Auschwitz. Once again, both the Jews and the Arabs of Palestine had a choice to make. For Haj Amin al-Husseini, the choice was clear and can be summed up as follows: the enemy of my enemy is my friend. The Germans were at war with the British and were hell-bent on annihilating the Jews. What better friends could the Mufti seek out than the Nazis?

For the Jews, the choice was not so straightforward and was articulated by Ben Gurion as follows: "We will fight with the British against Hitler as if there were no white paper, and we will fight the white paper as if there were no war." In November 1941, the *SS Struma* set sail from Rumania for Palestine packed with 769 Jews who were fleeing a nightmare that would come to be known as the Holocaust. The *Struma* was barely seaworthy and had to stop in Istanbul for major repairs. The Jews aboard ship begged the Turkish to grant them asylum, while the Jews of Palestine beseeched the British to allow them to come to Palestine. Both requests were refused, and shortly after the Turks had the *Struma* towed out of their harbor, the ship sank, drowning all those aboard, including 269 women and seventy children. Throughout the war, the British tried to keep Jewish immigration to a bare minimum while the Jews did everything they could to bring Jews illegally into Palestine. At the same time, thousands of Jews fought in both the British and U.S. armies against the Nazis, and, in 1944 a Jewish Brigade was formed in Palestine to fight alongside the British. In 1945, the 3,000-member Jewish Brigade was shipped to Italy for combat against the Germans. Their uniforms featured a blue-and-white Star of David. Many chose to also wear yellow armbands, like those that the Germans forced Jews to wear.

From Auschwitz to Independence

After the war, it was crystal clear to the Jews of Palestine that a sovereign Jewish state was an absolute imperative. The only question was how to deal with the British, and on this the community was split. Menachem Begin and his followers felt that if it would take a fight to get the British to leave so that the Jews could finally establish their state, then so be it. David Ben-Gurion and his followers were convinced that an armed conflict with the British would jeopardize further immigration and British support for a state, and that diplomacy was the way to achieve their goal. Each followed his own course. This led to a bitter split within the Jewish community and to Begin leading an underground Jewish militia beyond the purview of Ben Gurion and the Hagganah.* This force, the Irgun, launched numerous attacks against the British military in Palestine. Its most audacious act of all was directed against the British military command headquarters that were located in the majestic King David Hotel. On July 22, 1946, the Irgun planted explosives in the basement of the hotel. The British ignored the Irgun's warning to evacuate the building, and the ensuing blast killed ninety-one people and wounded forty-five.

By 1947, the British had finally had enough of Palestine and handed their headache over to the United Nations. The UN then created UNSCOP, the United Nations Special Committee on Palestine, to determine the fate of Palestine once and for all. UNSCOP, similar to the Peel Commission before it, concluded that partition was the only viable solution and proposed the following: (1) Palestine would be divided into two countries, one Arab and one Jewish. The Jewish state would have an Arab minority, and about 100,000 Jews would live in the Arab country. (2) Jerusalem would not be a part of either country and rather would have a special international status under UN auspices. (3) For the first two years, 150,000 Jews would be allowed to immigrate to the Jewish state, with the amount dropping to 60,000 annually after that. (4) An economic union between the two countries would be overseen by a nine-member board of three Jews, three Arabs, and three UN representatives. (5) The Jewish state would provide financial assistance to the Arab state. (See map on page 153.)

Once again, the Jews and the Arabs responded very differently to the partition plan. The Jews chose to accept partition and the creation of two states in western Palestine. The Arabs convened an emergency meeting of the Arab League in Lebanon and voted to totally reject partition and to begin supplying men and weapons to fight for the creation of an Arab state in all of Palestine. It wasn't long before fighting broke out between Jewish and Arab forces in Palestine. Soon,

---

*This split actually pre-dated Ben-Gurion and Begin and continues to echo in Israel today. People like Benjamin Netanyahu, Yitzchak Shamir, and Ariel Sharon have their roots in the Begin camp, while Shimon Peres, Yitzchak Rabin, and Ehud Barak look back to Ben-Gurion for inspiration.

Jerusalem was under siege and the Jewish residents and institutions in the city were cut off from the rest of the Jews in Palestine.

On April 13, 1948 a convoy of homemade armored cars and buses, carrying eighty civilians—most of them doctors and nurses, set out for Mount Scopus in Jerusalem, where Hebrew University and Hadassah Hospital were located. Arab forces ambushed the convoy just two hundred yards from a British military post. Despite requests to the British for help, the British did nothing. The doctors and nurses were outgunned and surrounded. Most were killed in the shooting that lasted for over three hours. The survivors were burned alive in their buses.

On May 11, a diminutive Golda Meyerson—originally from Milwaukee, Wisconsin—disguised herself as an Arab woman and set out for a secret meeting with King Abdullah of Transjordan. The two had met before and had established a congenial rapport. It was Mrs. Meyerson's perception, as well as the perception of other Jewish and Arab leaders, that King Abdullah believed that a way could be found for the Jews and the Arabs to live as neighbors. On that day in May, her mission was to dissuade the king from going to war. The king, for his part, told Mrs. Meyerson that it was impossible for him to break ranks with the other Arab leaders and he urged the Jews to postpone their declaration of independence. King Abdullah also had his eye on Jerusalem.

> *"I firmly believe that Divine Providence has restored you, a Semite people who were banished to Europe and have benefited from its progress, to the Semite east, which needs your knowledge and initiative...I deplore the coming bloodshed and destruction. Let us hope we shall meet again and will not sever our relations. If you find it necessary to meet me during the actual fighting, do not hesitate to come and see me."*
> King Abdullah to Golda Meyerson, May 11, 1948

Golda Meyerson (who later became Israeli Prime Minister Golda Meir), returned to Tel Aviv and reported her failure to David Ben-Gurion. Ben Gurion remained convinced that the opportune moment had arrived and was determined to proceed with the declaration.

May 14, 1948, was set as the date when the British would complete their withdrawal from Palestine. On May 13, the text of Israel's Declaration of Independence was completed. It included a call for peace that said:

"We extend our hand in peace and neighborliness to all the neighboring states and peoples, and invite them to cooperate with the independent Jewish nation for the common good of all. The State of Israel is prepared to make its contribution to the progress of the Middle East as a whole."

Just after breakfast on May 14, the British left Jerusalem—their three decades in the Holy Land were finished. By lunchtime that same day, a full-scale invasion by all the surrounding Arab armies was under way. At five o'clock that afternoon, David Ben-Gurion rose in the hall of the Tel Aviv museum to announce the creation of the State of Israel and to read aloud its Declaration of Independence:

"The Land of Israel was the birthplace of the Jewish people. Here their spiritual, religious and national identity was formed... Exiled from the Land of Israel the Jewish people remained faithful to it in all the countries of their dispersion, never ceasing to pray and hope for their return and the restoration of their national freedom. Jews strove throughout the centuries to go back to the land of their fathers and regain their statehood. In recent decades they returned in their masses. They sought peace, yet were prepared to defend themselves... We hereby proclaim the establishment of the Jewish State in Palestine, to be called Medinat Yisrael (The State of Israel). The State of Israel will be open to the immigration of Jews from all countries of their dispersion; will uphold the full social and political equality of all its citizens, without distinction of religion, race, or sex; will guarantee freedom of religion, conscience, education and culture; will safeguard the Holy Places of all religions. We extend our hand in peace and neighborliness to all the neighboring states and peoples... Our call goes out to the Jewish people all over the world to rally to our side in the task of immigration and development, and to stand by us in the great struggle for the fulfillment of the dream of generations for the redemption of Israel. With trust in the Rock of Israel, we set our hand to this declaration, on this Sabbath eve, the fifth of Iyar, 5708, the fourteenth of May, 1948."

Surprise, Surprise—Israel Survives

If you think the U.S. Olympic victory in hockey over Russia shocked the world, that was nothing compared to what happened in 1948. Many thought the Jews of Palestine were doomed.

In 1948, the Jews of Israel were outnumbered and undertrained, and had a deficiency of weaponry, almost no modern armored vehicles, and no air force. In many instances, concentration camp survivors who made their way to the fledgling state were given a weapon and rudimentary training and then sent to battle. The Arabs, though not the world's finest fighting force, were well-armed, possessed the armored weaponry and air force of a modern army, and had been trained by British officers. In many instances, British officers were on the ground to help guide the Arabs in their assault.

When the war ended, Israel emerged from battle wounded and battered but alive. Territorially, its borders exceeded what the partition plan had originally envisioned, and though still desperately vulnerable, it was slightly more defensible. In Jerusalem, the Jewish Quarter had been overrun by Jordanian forces, and the Old City, with all its Christian, Muslim, and Jewish holy places, was annexed by Jordan. That was the last Jews would see of the Western Wall for twenty years.* Throughout the war, the Israeli military had relied on flexibility, extensive night fighting, small, agile commando strikes, improvisation, bravery, and sheer will—not to mention divine assistance—to ensure Israel's survival. At war's end, 6,000 Jews had been killed. These deaths represented one percent of the population and was equivalent to the United States losing two and a half million people.

From February through July 1949, Israel negotiated separate armistice agreements with Egypt, Lebanon, Jordan, and Syria. These agreements were intended to be the forerunners of formal peace treaties, but the Arabs balked and this never came to be. Though the

---

*John Phillips writing in the June 7 and 28, 1948 issues of *Life Magazine* reported that on May 28, 1948, "Palestinian hangers-on burst in and reduced [the Jewish Quarter] to smoking ruin after the beaten Jews gave in. Had any Jew decided to remain in the Old City he would have probably been dead by nightfall." Indeed, the Arabs blew-up almost every synagogue and school in the Jewish Quarter. Remaining synagogues were desecrated and subsequently used as horse stables and refuse dumps. Jews were permanently barred from entering the Old City and visiting the Western Wall, the ancient Mount of Olives cemetery, or any other Jewish holy sites. The Jordanians also took gravestones from the Mount of Olives and used them in construction projects.

Jewish State of Israel had become a reality, for the next three decades the Arabs would insist that Israel lacked even the basic right to exist. Indeed, those three decades would be one long Arab effort to bring the Jewish state to its knees.

Before moving on to the ensuing three decades of war, we will first look at two highly contentious issues related to Israel's birth and the 1948 War of Independence. The first is the displacement of the Arab population of Palestine prior to the war, and the second is the refugee problem that was a result of the war.

This Town Ain't Big Enough For The Both of Us: The Big Myth

A myth that has become accepted as common knowledge goes like this: The Jewish effort to populate Palestine necessarily involved the depopulation of its age-old Palestinian Arab community. Thus, the more the Jews came, built, and developed, the more the Arabs were displaced, and the worse off they became.

Nothing could be further from the truth. Let's take a look.

1. When the Muslims first conquered Palestine in 638, the inhabitants of the land were primarily Christians and Jews. At that time, Arabs lived in Arabia (Saudi Arabia), and the conquest of Palestine was just one piece of a much broader series of conquests. Following the Muslim conquest, no attempt was made to impose an Islamic or Arab identity on Palestine, and no significant influx of Arabs into the land occurred.

> *"During the first century after the Arab conquest the caliph and governors of Syria and the land [Palestine] ruled almost entirely over Christian and Jewish subjects. Apart from the Bedouin, in the earliest days the only Arabs west of the Jordan were the garrison."*
>
> Reverend James W. Parkes, *Whose Land? A History of the People of Palestine*

Over the centuries, Palestine's primary attraction was as a place of pilgrimage. Christians from around the world came to visit the holy sites of Christianity, and many ended up staying. For Muslims who were unable to make the Hajj to Mecca, Jerusalem sometimes became a place of secondary pilgrimage.* Palestine, due to frequent invasions, coupled with it being a place of pilgrimage, became a land whose population reflected a vast mix of ethnic origins.

> *"Among the people who have long been counted as 'indigenous Palestinian Arabs' are Balkans, Syrians, Latins, Egyptians, Turks, Armenians, Italians, Persians, Kurds, Afghans, Sudanese, Algerians, and Tartars."*
>
> Joan Peters, *From Time Immemorial*

2. By the year 1500, almost nine hundred years had passed since the first Arab conquest, and in all of Palestine there were only 49,000 families representing a total population of 200,000. Two hundred thousand is not even a third of the population of Jerusalem today and is less than a quarter of the present population of Amman, Jordan. When the Ottoman Empire arrived in 1517, it had been fifteen centuries since the destruction of the Temple and the dispersion of the Jews. Throughout that entire period, though Palestine became religiously significant to both Christianity and Islam, its population was always in a great state of flux, and no distinctly recognizable ethnic group considered the area of Palestine to be their natural or ancestral homeland. The closest anyone came to establishing any kind of independent presence in the land were European Catholics who established the Latin Kingdom of Jerusalem during the Crusader period.

3. The years 1800-1840 were a time of upheaval for the population of Palestine. During that period, Palestine was invaded by both Napoleon and the Egyptians. From 1831 to 1840, Palestine was ruled by Muhammad Ali (no, not the boxer) of Egypt.

> *"The conquest did establish law and order in the country, but caused many old inhabitants to flee and new elements to settle in the land... the Egyptian settlers scattered to many urban and rural points, appropriated large tracts of land, and lent variety and numbers to the existing population... According to the*

---

*Muslims are required to make, once in their lives, a pilgrimage, or Hajj, to Mecca. Jerusalem is not considered to be a substitute destination, and Islamic authorities often opposed pilgrimage to Jerusalem as a slight to Mecca.

*British Palestine Exploration Fund regional map of Jaffa, most
of the city was made up of Egyptian populated districts."*
Arieh L. Avneri, The Claim of Dispossession

Additionally, throughout the mid-1800s, incessant little wars
broke out between villages and rival clans in Palestine. It was often the
case that one village would decimate another, destroy their property
and cultivated acreage, and drive the inhabitants into exile.

4. The century from 1850 to 1948 is fascinating, significant, and
telling. We have already looked at this period from the point of view of
the development of Zionism, the return of the Jews to Israel, and the
British mandate. We are now going to look at the population of Palestine
during this pre-state century, and consider the implications that
population had for the birth of Israel. First we'll look at the numbers,
and then we'll explain them.

(Note: The figures for the Arab population include both Muslims
and Christians. Christians were about 8-10 percent of the total, but for
our purpose it's easier to just view them together.)

Year	Arab Population	Jewish Population
1600	250,000	5,000
1850	480,000	17,000
1890	530,000	43,000
1922	590,000	84,000
1931	760,000	174,000
1939	900,000	450,000
1948	980,000	650,000
1954	192,000	1,530,000
1969	423,000	2,500,000
1989	843,000	3,700,000
1997	1,120,000	4,640,000

From 1850 until 1948, the Arab population of Palestine doubled,
while the Jewish population increased forty times. Leaving birthrates
aside, the question is this: What transformed Palestine, for the first time
in almost twenty decades, from a place of limited, unstable, and
fluctuating population to the hottest new suburb in the Middle East?
The answer for both the Jews and Arabs is the same: immigration. The
stimulus for immigration, however, was drastically different. The Jews

came to Palestine to rebuild their homeland, and the Arabs came because Jewish development (along with British development after World War I) created a whole new economic reality filled with unprecedented opportunities. As the British and the Jews built new infrastructure in Palestine, as the business sector began to grow, and as the Jews developed an agricultural economy that went way beyond subsistence to export, Arabs flowed into the area in search of employment, stability, and opportunity. In addition to a surge in the agricultural sector, between 1917 and 1947 over 140,000 Arabs were employed by the British government in Palestine. Similarly, as the Jewish people further developed and modernized the economy and the country, the quality of life dramatically increased throughout Palestine.

"The Arab population of Palestine was small and limited until Jewish resettlement restored the barren lands and drew to it Arabs from neighboring countries... the Arab population in recent decades were recent newcomers—either late immigrants or descendants of persons who had immigrated into Palestine in the previous seventy years."

Dr. Carl Herman Voss, 1953
Voss was chairman of the American Christian Palestine Committee.

"The Jewish-generated economic boom prompted Arab in-migration and immigration into the Jewish settled areas of Western Palestine beginning in the 1870s and continuing throughout the British administration of Palestine until 1946 or 1947."

Joan Peters, *From Time Immemorial*

"During those twenty-four years [1922–1946] approximately 100,000 Arabs entered the country from neighboring lands. The influx could be traced in some measure to the orderly government provided by the British; but far more, certainly, to the economic opportunities made possible by Jewish settlement... by opening new markets for Arab produce and new employment opportunities for Arab labor."

Howard M. Sachar, *A History of Israel*

"The most profitable branch in agriculture between the two World Wars was citriculture. The other branch of intensive

agriculture in the expanding economy was the growing of vegetables. In 1922 Arab farmers cultivated 30,000 dunam [7,500 acres] and produced 20,000 tons of vegetables. In 1944/45 Arabs farmed 239,733 dunam [60,000 acres] and supplied 189,804 tons of vegetables to the market. In 1931, there were 339 factories owned by Arabs and in 1942—1,558 factories. The rapid development of the Arab economy, with a concomitant rise in the standard of living, gave rise to demands for a higher quality of health and educational services. As a result, health facilities were expanded, and the scope and level of educational opportunities were also far beyond those prevailing in the neighboring Arab countries."

Arieh L. Avneri, *The Claim of Dispossession*

"As the most visible Arab-American critic of Yasser Arafat, I get a lot of hate mail... Let me state this plainly and clearly: The Jews in Israel took no one's land. As the Jews came, something interesting happened. Arabs followed. I don't blame them. They came for jobs. They came for prosperity. They came for freedom. And they came in large numbers."

Joseph Farrah, *WorldNetDaily.com*, April 23, 2002
Joseph Farrah is a columnist for the international edition of *The Jerusalem Post*, and founding editor of *WorldNetDaily.com*.

For the sake of perspective, we should not forget the basic fact that from 1917 to 1948 the British kept tight controls over Jewish immigration to Palestine, while there were virtually no restrictions on Arab immigration.

The truth about Jewish emigration to Palestine is that not only did the Jews not displace a large indigenous Arab population that had been there for millennia but that it was Jewish efforts to develop Palestine that directly resulted in a dramatic rise in Palestine's Arab population. It wouldn't be true to say that there weren't Jews who, as statehood approached—and particularly after the Arab riots in the twenties and thirties—hoped that a way could be found to establish a Jewish state that had as few Arab citizens as possible. Nonetheless, it was never a matter of policy or practice for the burgeoning Jewish community in Palestine to seek to drive the Arabs out of their homes.

As we have seen, the Arabs repeatedly rejected the option of living in peace with their Jewish neighbors and instead opted for war. This brings us to the issue of Palestinian refugees.

Will the Real Refugees Please Stand Up?

After the survival of Israel, the next major outcome of the war in '48 was the creation of hundreds of thousands of Arab refugees. The actual number of refugees is impossible to determine (estimates run from 400,000 to 800,000) and remains a question of historical debate. What isn't debatable, though, is the fact that those people who became refugees were not a unified people with a common sense of identity, rooted in a shared land, who shared a common history stretching back over the centuries. Rather, a huge proportion of the Arabs living in Palestine when the war began in 1948 were recent arrivals with no sense of distinctly Palestinian identity or nationhood.*

> *"By 1947 much of the Palestinian Arab population had only an indistinct, if any, idea of national purpose and statehood. Most Palestinian Arabs had no sense of separate national or cultural identity to distinguish them from, say, the Arabs of Syria, Lebanon or Egypt."*
>
> Benny Morris, *The Birth of the Palestinian Refugee Problem, 1947-1949*

The fact that so many Arabs living in Palestine were recent immigrants was deliberately ignored by the UN when it created the United Nations Relief and Works Agency for Palestine (UNRWA) in 1949. Through the UNRWA, the UN dealt with (and continues to deal with) the Arab refugees much differently than it ever did with other refugees in the world. All other refugees are aided by the United Nations High Commissioner for Refugees—the UNHCR. Unlike the UNHCR, the UNRWA criteria used to determine refugee status declared that anyone living in Palestine for two years before the War of Independence was a refugee. Nowhere else in the world has the UN lowered the defining threshold of a refugee so radically. Also, Arab refugees are the only people in the world whose children and grand-children inherit refugee status. This explains why the Palestinians are

---

*The development of a specifically Palestinian identity is dealt with on pp. 82-83. The specifics of where the refugees went and their fate after the war is examined on pp. 85-87.

the only refugee population in the world that increases in number from year to year. Additionally, all other refugee populations are defined as people who face "a well-founded fear of being persecuted," and no such fear can be applied to the Arabs who lived in Palestine.

Today, if you listen to media reports or to PLO demands for a Palestinian "right of return," you will hear that there are four to five million Palestinian refugees. What you don't hear is that, if the Arabs were dealt with in the same way the UNHCR has dealt with tens of millions of other refugees, less than a million of them—most of whom are in Syria and Lebanon—could possibly be considered refugees.

> *"While I was examining United Nations data from 1948 onward, a seemingly casual alteration of the definition of what constitutes an Arab "refugee" from Israel caught my attention. In other cases the more or less universally used description of eligibility included those people who were forced to leave "permanent" or "habitual" homes. In the case of the Arab refugees, however, the definition had been broadened to include any persons who had been in Palestine for only two years before Israel's statehood in 1948."*
>
> Joan Peters, *From Time Immemorial*

In a nutshell, here's what happened in Palestine between 1900 and 1948:

Large numbers of Jews immigrated to Palestine and brought extensive economic development with them. As a result, Arabs also immigrated in large numbers and reaped the benefits of Jewish devotion to and development of the land. Eventually, the Arabs turned around and said to the Jews—"Thanks for the new country; now get out of here." And then it happened again. In 1948, after the Jews refused to get out or be thrown out, the Arabs once again turned to the Jews and said, in effect, "You know, Palestine was really ours all along. Then you Jewish colonialists stole it and drove us out, and now we want it back." Go figure.

From War to War to War

In the Arab world, the failure to overrun the Jews was seen as a catastrophe. Israelis hoped that, as time passed, the Arabs would come to accept their place in the Middle East and that eventually begrudging acceptance would give way to pragmatic coexistence. For the Arabs, the failure to vanquish the Jews was a humiliation that simply had to be undone. We will now take a brief look at the three major wars that followed Israel's survival in 1948, and then proceed to taking a closer look at the issue of the Palestinians.

1956: The Sinai War

Egypt, in violation of the armistice agreement with Israel, closed the Suez Canal to Israeli shipping in 1949. This was a clear sign of problems to come.

In 1952, Colonel Gamal Abdel Nasser led a military coup that drove King Farouk from power in Egypt. Nasser had a Pan-Arabic, nationalist dream—he aimed to become the preeminent leader of a united Islamic world, and Israel was the perfect foil for his ambitions.

After the war of '48, because Egypt controlled the Sinai Peninsula as well as the Gaza Strip, it was able to station troops along Israel's southern border. After coming to power, Nasser followed a policy of launching raids into Israel. These raids targeted civilians and resulted in a very difficult state of affairs for Jews living in southern Israel. Hundreds were killed and wounded. In 1955, the Soviet Union—via Czechoslovakia—began to supply Egypt with large quantities of advanced arms and equipment. In July 1956, Egypt nationalized the Suez Canal and blockaded the Strait of Tiran. Israel's access to Africa and Asia was crippled. In October, the Egyptian army began taking up positions in the Negev. That same month, Egypt signed a tripartite agreement that made Nasser commander of joint Egyptian-Syrian-Jordanian forces.

> *"Egypt has decided to dispatch her heroes, the disciples of Pharaoh and the sons of Islam and they will cleanse the land of Palestine. We demand vengeance, and vengeance is Israel's death… Our hatred is very strong. There is no sense in talking about peace with Israel."*
>
> Egyptian President Gamal Abdel Nasser, 1955-56

Israel felt isolated and threatened. Soon, Israel came to the conclusion that Nasser was determined to launch an all-out war, so Prime Minister David Ben-Gurion and his government made the decision to strike first.* On October 29, 1956, Israel launched a paratroop attack against Egyptian forces in the Sinai. By November 5, Israel occupied the entire Sinai and ended the blockade of the Strait of Tiran. The war ended on November 6 with a UN-sponsored cease-fire. Eventually, under heavy pressure from the United States, Israel was forced to relinquish all the territory it had captured. In return, the United Nations placed peace-keeping troops in the Sinai as a buffer between Egypt and Israel. The Strait of Tiran would remain open to Israeli shipping until Nasser decided to close it once again in 1967—thus paving the way for the Six-Day War.

From the Brink of Despair: The Six-Day War

"The liquidation of Israel will not be realized through a declaration of war against Israel by Arab states, but Arab unity and inter-Arab understanding will serve as a hangman's rope for Israel."
Official Egyptian newspaper, *Al-Akhbar*, April 4, 1963

"We shall never call for nor accept peace. We have resolved to drench this land with our blood, to oust you, aggressors, and throw you into the sea for good."
Syrian Defense Minister, Hafez Assad, May 24, 1966
Assad would later become the dictatorial President of Syria.

Imagine what it felt like to be a Jew in Israel in the spring of 1967. Mothers and fathers, grandmothers and grandfathers converged on schoolyards across the country. No, they weren't there to watch a graduation ceremony but to dig trenches and fill sandbags. They had already secured their homes as best they could; their basements became air-raid shelters, car headlights were painted blue so they would be less visible at night, and now they all helped to fortify the schools. Hotels were equipped for use as huge first-aid centers and stockpiles of plastic sheeting were readied for wrapping corpses. Public parks were consecrated by rabbis and designated for use as cemeteries. The streets at night were empty.

---

*Please note: A discussion of British and French involvement in this war is beyond the scope of this work.

"Each day seemed to contain double the number of hours, and each hour seemed endless. It was as though some gigantic clock was clicking away for all of us, though no one except Nasser knew when the zero hour would be."

Golda Meir

In the spring of 1967, Israel stood at the threshold of war, and everyone knew what that meant. For the first time in its history, the prime minister, Levi Eshkol, invited the leader of the opposition, Menachem Begin, to join him in a government of national unity.

On May 15, Egypt began massing its forces along Israel's southern border. It was along this front that Israel was least prepared to fight. The UN forces stationed there since 1956 were supposed to ensure that the Sinai not be used as a launching pad for an assault on Israel. The following day, Egypt demanded that the UN remove its forces from the Sinai, and Secretary General U Thant complied. A few days later, Syrian troops were poised for attack along the Golan Heights overlooking the north of Israel. Iraq too was readying to join the invasion. On May 22, Egypt once again closed the Strait of Tiran, crippling Israel's trade and supply route to the east and cutting off her supply of oil from Iran. Since 1956, the United States, Great Britain, Canada, and France had assured Israel that they would guarantee Israel's right of passage through the Strait—but they did nothing.

On May 23, Prime Minister Eshkol convened an emergency meeting of his cabinet and military leaders. Abba Eban, Israel's foreign minister at that time, later reflected on his drive from Jerusalem to Tel Aviv for that meeting—"I was gripped by a sharp awareness of the fragility of all cherished things. Our minds revolved around the question of survival; so it must have been in ancient days, with Babylon or Assyria at the gates." Following the meeting, military chief of staff General Yitzchak Rabin suffered a nervous breakdown. Five days later, Eshkol addressed the country. His tone was somber, and he seemed tentative and even at a loss for words. His speech left people hanging between despair, panic, and prayer. Jews in the United States, and around the world, watched with a sense of helplessness as a ring of enemies closed in on Israel. Synagogues filled as if it were Yom Kippur—and Jews prayed. Soviet propaganda assured its people, including millions of Jews, that the end of Israel was at hand.

In the Sinai, Israel faced 120,000 troops and 900 tanks. Egypt had an additional 100,000 troops and 300 tanks in place if they were needed.

On the Golan, Israel faced 75,000 troops and 400 tanks. Iraq was moving its forces into Jordan and together they had another 40,000 troops and 450 tanks. The combined Arab air forces had over 700 planes. In mid-May, Israel began a massive call-up of reservists that left its cities virtually empty of fighting-age men. Fully mobilized, Israel could throw 250,000 soldiers into battle. It had 800 tanks and 300 airplanes.

> *"We were waiting for the day when we would be fully prepared and confident. Recently we felt we are strong enough, that if we were to enter a battle with Israel, with God's help, we could triumph. I know what we have here in Egypt and what Syria has. I also know that other Arab states—Iraq, for instance, has sent its troops to Syria; Algeria will send troops; Kuwait also will send troops. This is Arab power."*
>
> Egyptian President Nasser,
> May 26, 1967

With its back against the wall and with hundreds of thousands of women and children at home not knowing what would happen to their husbands and fathers who were now poised to defend Israel, Israel made the fateful decision to strike first.

The Six-Day War was launched by Israel on June 5, 1967. For all intents and purposes, the war was over in three hours. A brilliantly executed aerial attack caught the Arabs completely off guard. Their entire air forces were destroyed before they could even get any of their planes off the ground. With air superiority assured, the Israeli forces had gained a decisive advantage. While a number of terrible battles lay ahead, victory had been virtually assured once the Israelis had won that advantage.

By the time the war was over, Israel had again captured the entire Sinai Peninsula, as well as the Golan Heights and the West Bank, but the emotional climax of the war came in Jerusalem. On the morning of June 7, Israeli forces reached the Temple Mount. For the first time in two decades, a shofar was sounded at the Western Wall, and for the first time in nearly two thousand years, Jerusalem was under Jewish sovereignty. Rabbi Shlomo Goren chanted the prayer for those who had fallen in defense of Israel, as battle-weary soldiers clutched the ancient stones of the Wall. Tears poured from their eyes.

Golda Meir's words echoed the collective relief of an entire people. Reflecting on the moment when she heard about the successful attack on the Arab air forces, she said, "I stood alone at the door of my house, looked up at the cloudless, undisturbed sky, and realized that we had been rescued from the terrible fear that had haunted us all. There would still be death and mourning and misery. But the planes that had been readied to bomb us were all mortally crippled. I stood there and breathed in the night air as though I had not drawn a really deep breath for weeks."

On June 10, a UN-sponsored cease-fire took effect. Israel's stunning victory had cost her families 777 dead and 2,586 wounded and crippled. Proportionally, this was twice what the United States lost in the Vietnam War.

1973: From Khartoum to Yom Kippur

Two weeks after the end of the Six-Day War, the Israeli cabinet met to discuss what it believed would be imminent peace negotiations with the Arabs. The cabinet voted unanimously to return both the Sinai Peninsula as well as the Golan Heights in return for signed peace treaties that included the demilitarization of those areas. As Moshe Dayan put it, Israel was waiting for a phone call from Arab leaders to commence peace negotiations. Not only did that phone call never come, but the Arabs cut the lines altogether. On August 29, the leaders of thirteen Arab countries convened the Khartoum Conference and issued a joint declaration featuring three no's:

> "Kings and presidents have agreed... **no** peace with Israel, **no** negotiations with Israel, **no** recognition of Israel."
> Khartoum Conference Declaration, September 1, 1967

In September 1973, six years after the Khartoum Conference, both Egypt and Syria were again massing huge numbers of men and arms along their borders with Israel. The Soviet Union had supplied the Arabs with a vast amount of weaponry, a huge number of its most sophisticated anti-aircraft missiles, and a strategy designed to neutralize Israel's air superiority. At the same time, the Arabs implemented a highly effective misinformation campaign.

Israeli intelligence and the Cabinet of Prime Minister Golda Meir were monitoring the situation closely. In early October, intelligence officials made a presentation to the military leadership and characterized the possibility of war as "the lowest of the low." The consensus was that while Egypt was clearly preparing for war, it was still two years away from being able to launch a serious attack.

On the night of October 5, Israel came to a virtual standstill. It was the eve of Yom Kippur—the holiest day in the Jewish year—and the Jews of Israel were going to synagogue for the Kol Nidre service. That evening, as Jews around the world began their day of fasting and prayer, the tides and currents in the Suez Canal were just where they needed to be should an army decide to cross. In fact, such a decision had already been made.

By Yom Kippur morning, cars were pulling up to synagogues across Israel with emergency mobilization orders for tens of thousands of soldiers. War had arrived.

By 2:00 that afternoon—

"Two hundred and forty Egyptian aircraft crossed the Canal. Simultaneously, 2,000 guns opened up along the entire front. In the first minute of attack, 10,500 shells fell on Israeli positions at a rate of 175 shells per second. Over 30,000 tons of concentrated destruction turned the entire East Bank of the Suez Canal into an inferno for fifty-three minutes. The full impact of the Egyptian crossing fell upon a total of 436 Israeli soldiers and three tanks actually on the waterfront. They were men of the Jerusalem Brigade, serving their annual reserve duty. Because Jerusalem had absorbed a large proportion of new immigrants of late, many were inexperienced soldiers with little or no battle experience."

Chaim Herzog, *The Arab-Israeli Wars*

Egyptian military planners had estimated that the crossing of the Suez would result in as many as 10,000 Egyptians being killed. By the end of the day, Egypt had lost only 208 soldiers. Meanwhile, simultaneous with the Egyptian attack in the south, Syria unleashed a massive attack in the north. The Syrian forces were comprised of 1,400 tanks. Their mission was to overrun the Golan Heights within thirty-six hours and then to begin an invasion of the Galilee. Once the invasion was completed, Haifa, Israel's third largest city, would be within striking distance. The largest Syrian attack force was comprised of 600 tanks. Against these 600 tanks, Israel had 57 tanks ready to do battle. The Israeli armored division on the Golan was under the command of General Rafael Eitan. His orders were simple. "Hold back the Syrian advance as long as you can!"

Israel's situation on the Golan quickly became desperate, and it would take extraordinary efforts to slow the Syrian attack—efforts like those of Zvi "Tzvika" Greengold:

> *"On Yom Kippur morning Zvi Greengold was given three tanks that were quickly taken out of the repair workshop and was ordered to lead them in a holding action. After a short time, Tzvika saw the first line of Syrian tanks. He fired a shell from close range and the tank caught on fire. The force of the explosion put out the communications system in Tzvika's tank. Tzvika signaled with his hand to the commander of one of the other two tanks to move closer to him. The two of them exchanged tanks, and Tzvika ordered the commander of the second tank to follow him and do exactly what he did. After he had destroyed ten more tanks, the Syrians assumed they had encountered a large Israeli force and retreated. In the meantime, reserve units began to arrive. They managed to hold the Syrians for a few more hours. But in the early hours of the morning they entered the range of Syrian artillery and went up in flames. At the last minute, Tzvika and his crew jumped out of their tank and rolled into a ditch while putting out the flames on their clothes. He woke up just in time and managed to find the tank of the deputy brigade commander and continued fighting at his side."*
>
> Ehud Barak, from the anthology, *Lionhearts: Heroes of Israel*

On Sunday, October 7, Tzvika Greengold was wounded in battle and taken to a hospital. A week later he ran away from the hospital to rejoin the fighting on the Golan Heights.

In the days following the initial attacks by Egypt and Syria, Israel's situation was perilous. Jews everywhere held their breath and fought to hold back the tears. It was only after Israel successfully launched major counter-offensives that it was able to push back the forces that had come ominously close to advancing on its major urban centers.

Two weeks after the war began, and only after Israel engaged Egypt in the second largest tank battle in history, a cease fire was announced. On October 24, in the middle of the holiday of *Sukkot*, the war came to an end. In the Yom Kippur War, Israel had faced a near-fatal situation and had been spared the worst. Nonetheless, Israel had lost 2,569 men, and another 7,500 were wounded—triple the losses Israel had suffered in the Six-Day War. In the aftermath of the war, Israel's morale was deeply shaken, and there was a crisis of confidence in the government for not having been properly prepared.

Camp David: Peace at Last

The goal of the Arabs at the outset of the Yom Kippur war was to at the very least undo the consequences of the Six-Day War. By inflicting punishing blows and heavy losses on Israel, the Arabs had hoped that Israel would agree to withdraw from territories it had captured in 1967, even without gaining the full peace it desired. The Arabs were also counting on the United States and the Soviet Union to put great pressure on Israel for the sake of stability in the region, even if formal peace remained unrealized. They were partially successful.

In November of 1977, after extensive behind-the-scenes preparations, the announcement was made that Egyptian President Anwar Sadat would visit Israel and address the Knesset. I remember what it was like in Jerusalem on the night that Sadat arrived. Though there were soldiers on every corner, the streets were virtually empty because everyone was at home watching a historic event unfold before their eyes. When Sadat disembarked from his plane, he was greeted by Prime Minister Menachem Begin, virtually the entire Israeli cabinet and a country that was tasting unprecedented hope. Golda Meir had been prime minister when Sadat launched the Yom Kippur War. On the tarmac of the airport she took Sadat's hand and said, "We've been waiting for you for a long time." Sadat's response was, "The time has come."

Ten months later, President Jimmy Carter helped bring Begin, Sadat and their advisors together at Camp David in the hills of Maryland for another historic meeting. On September 17, 1978, the Camp David Peace Accords between Israel and Egypt were signed by Anwar Sadat, Menachem Begin, and Jimmy Carter. Israel had agreed to return the entire Sinai Peninsula, Egypt agreed to peace, and the world applauded a historic event. In the Arab world, though, Egypt was ostracized for having made the traitorous move of breaking ranks and signing its own accord with Israel.

Twenty-two years after the Israeli-Egyptian peace agreement, Camp David would once again figure prominently in the Arab-Israeli conflict. We will get to that soon, but first we need to meet the Palestinians.

Palestinians, Arabs, Arafat, *and Israel*

5

The Palestinian people define themselves as those Arabs who were living permanently in Palestine prior to 1947. Palestinian identity is passed from father to child, and the vast majority of Palestinians are Muslim Arabs, though there are Christian Palestinian Arabs as well. While possessing a specific sub-identity, Palestinians view themselves and their destiny as an integral part of a larger Arab nation that transcends national borders and political affiliations.

> *"All Palestinians know that their principal constituency is Arab and that their struggle exists in an overwhelmingly Arab and Islamic environment."*
>
> Edward W. Said, *The Question of Palestine*

In today's world, the Palestinians are a people that claims that Palestine is rightfully theirs, that they were victimized by Western colonialism and Zionism, and that they were forcibly exiled from their ancestral homeland. The Palestinians view the liberation of Palestine not only as a Palestinian cause but as an Arab and Islamic cause as well. It is as Arabs and Muslims that Palestinians view the existence of Israel not only as a violation of Palestinian rights but as an intolerable invasion of a foreign element into the heartland of the Arab world.

> *"Palestine is the homeland of the Palestine Arab people and an integral part of the great Arab homeland, and the people of Palestine is a part of the Arab nation. The endeavor and effort of the Arab nation to liberate Palestine follows from this connection. The people of Palestine assumes its vanguard role in realizing this sacred national aim."*
>
> Palestinian National Covenant, Charter of the PLO
> Ratified in 1964 and revised in 1968

Regarding the future, Palestinians are divided into two camps: (1) those who adhere to the view that the total destruction of Israel and its replacement by a Palestinian state is the only way justice can be done for the egregiousness of Jewish sins and the only way that Palestinian rights can be realized and dignity restored and (2) those who feel that as long as a viable Palestinian state is created (even if it is comprised of less territory than it should be) that this would be an acceptable, though less than perfect, way of righting the wrongs of history.

The current conflict between Israelis and Palestinians is often characterized as the struggle of two small people over one very small piece of land. In fact, while this is true in the narrow sense, Palestinians —like all Arabs—have always viewed the conflict as a wider struggle between the Arab nation as a whole and the Jewish State of Israel. From the perspective of Israel, while the focus of its struggles of late has been primarily with the Palestinians, since its inception it has had to confront virtually the entire Arab world. While this chapter will deal primarily with the Palestinians in the context of the ongoing Arab-Israeli conflict, it will be helpful to take a look at the history of the relationship of the Arabs, Muslims, and others to the strip of land called Israel.

As is often the case with Israel, we're going to start our survey a long time ago.

Cannanites, Phoenicians, Philistines, and Israel

Let's begin by going back thirty-six hundred years, to about the year 1600 B.C.E. This will bring us to a time just prior to Abraham's relocation from Mesopotamia to Israel. Little is known of what was taking place in Arabia at that point in history (Arabia being the area that would eventually give rise to the Arab world). It would take another two thousand years for Islam to be born and another thirteen hundred years after that until anyone would hear of the Palestinian people.

"This short causeway along the eastern Mediterranean between Egypt and present-day Turkey was the scene of an astonishing and productive mixture of peoples and cultures. They came from all directions. The settled inhabitants of Syria and Palestine were known as Canaanites from about 1600 b.c.e. Almost certainly they did not constitute a single race but were formed through a mingling of peoples, some of whom came from the sea and some from the desert. They never created a powerful imperial state of their own; they submitted to the successive waves of conquerors, paid them tribute and traded with them."

Peter Mansfield, *A History of the Middle East*

By the time Abraham's grandson Jacob was a grown man, around the year 1400 B.C.E., much of what is today the western coast of Israel and Lebanon came under the dominion of the Phoenicians, a seafaring people from the western Mediterranean. While Phoenician trading outposts were prominent along the coast, the bulk of the inland region of Syria and Israel remained populated by nomadic tribes, small agrarian villages, and mini-kingdoms. By the time the Jewish people left Egypt and began their settlement of Israel in 1272 B.C.E., the region was home to at least seven separate mini-kingdoms including Edom, Moab, Ammon, and others. With the establishment of a constitutional monarchy under King Saul and King David, and with the completion of the first Temple in Jerusalem under King Solomon in 825 B.C.E., the land of Israel became home to a full-fledged nation for the first, and only, time in its history—at least until the establishment of the State of Israel in 1948.

So What About the Arabs?

Arab history can be most broadly divided into two eras; pre-Muhammad and post-Muhammad. The appearance of Muhammad, and the dramatic spread of Islam across the Arabian peninsula and beyond, is a clear historical watershed. The birth of Islam was more than the birth of a religion; it was the birth of an empire that would forever transform the Arabs and their history, world history, and the history of the land of Israel as well.

To understand the pre-Muhammad roots of the Arab people, I suggest you get a good map of the world and drive out to the middle of the closest desert. If there is no desert in your area, then your imagination will have to suffice.

Look for Saudi Arabia on your map. What you will notice is that Saudi Arabia occupies the vast majority of a huge peninsula that is home to the largest continuous sand desert on the face of the earth. To the south and east of Saudi Arabia, you will notice countries like Yemen, Oman, Qatar, Bahrain, and Kuwait. Up until ninety years ago, and for millennia before that, none of these countries existed. Rather, what existed was a vast desert sea populated by nomadic tribes, small farming villages where agriculture was possible, and settlements that grew up around oases. In that period, no sense of any unifying trans-Arabian identity existed; instead, people were identified by extended family loyalties and tribal ties.

> *"The inhabitants of Arabia, known as Arabs, comprised both nomads and settled townsfolk. The desert nomads, known as Bedouins, eked out a living by herding sheep, goats, and camels. The townspeople in Arabia were richer than the Bedouins and lived in settlements of mudbrick and stone. The Bedouins were believed to be the keepers of true Arabian culture. Everywhere, Arabian society was organized into tribes and clans. Arabia was a land of mixed religions and cultures."*
> Jonathan Bloom and Sheila Blair, *Islam*

> *"The dominant feature of the population of central and northern Arabia in this crucial period immediately preceding the rise of Islam is Bedouin tribalism... The only exception to this nomadic way of life was the oasis. Here small sedentary communities formed a rudimentary political organization and the outstanding family of the oasis would usually establish a kind of petty kingdom over its inhabitants."*
> Bernard Lewis, *The Arabs in History*

And Then Along Came Muhammad

Muhammad, known to Muslims as simply "the Prophet," was born around the year 570—six hundred years after Jesus and twenty-three hundred years after Abraham. Muhammad was an orphan who became a merchant and eventually married a wealthy and prominent woman from Mecca whose name was Khadija. Twenty years after their marriage, and after having four daughters, Muhammad began to have what he believed were prophetic visions. In these visions, the angel Gabriel revealed God's truth to Muhammad and eventually instructed him to begin a career of preaching that truth to others. Meccan society was polytheistic, and, beyond being objects of worship, the various gods and goddesses played a role in the business life of Mecca. Muhammad soon attracted a number of followers, but his sect's rejection of paganism was viewed as a potential threat to the stability of traditional Meccan society.

In 622, Muhammad and his followers were forced to flee Mecca for the settled area around the oasis of Yathrib. This oasis town eventually became known as Medina, "city of the prophet." In addition to pagan Arab tribe people, Christians and Jews also lived in Medina. In an effort to win Jewish adherents, Muhammad had his followers pray toward Jerusalem. When his religious overtures were rebuffed, Muhammad and his followers proceeded to change their direction of prayer to Mecca. In Medina, the primary economic activities were caravan raiding, warfare, and plundering. Soon, Muhammad not only had a substantial number of followers but was also a military leader in his own right. In 629, Muhammad set out for Mecca at the head of a large and fearsome army. Mecca surrendered without a fight. Once Mecca was his, instead of plundering the city, Muhammad ordered the removal of pagan idols and dedicated the Kaaba (the great black stone shrine) to Allah. Thus was Islam born.

Jerusalem and the Muslim Dynasties

Muhammad was an inspired religious leader, fervently devoted to winning over others to pure monotheism. He was also a politician and a successful general. The religion that he founded, Islam, contains all of these elements—monotheistic fervor, a complete mingling of religion and politics, and holy wars. Though Muhammad died suddenly in 632, the Islamic armies of his successors enabled Islam to conquer vast amounts of territory in an astonishingly short period of time. By the year 750, Islam was in control of all of Persia (Iran), the entire Arabian peninsula, the Middle East, much of North Africa, and Spain.

The first great Islamic dynasty was that of the Umayyads. In the year 637, the Umayyads conquered Jerusalem. The Umayyad rulers established what became the mold for Islam's relationship to Jerusalem. While Jerusalem was venerated as an ancient center of spirituality and eventually became significant to Muslim spirituality as well, in temporal terms it was never an important Muslim city.* None of the Muslim dynasties ever established a capital in Jerusalem, and it was often allowed to fall into disrepair.

The Umayyads established their capital in Damascus and decided to govern the general area of Palestine from a regional administrative capital in Ramallah instead of Jerusalem. When the Abassid dynasty defeated the Umayyads in 750, Jerusalem's status in the Islamic world declined even further. The Abbasids established their capital in Baghdad and ruled for almost five hundred years. Throughout the entire period, they paid little attention to Jerusalem, never seeking to make it an important Arab center and looking at it as little more than a place from which to collect taxes from the Christians and Jews who lived there.

> "Of the thirty-seven caliphs of the five hundred year old Abbasid dynasty, only two ever visited Jerusalem. The Abbasids largely ignored Jerusalem, but they were willing to repair monuments. Few new mosques were built in Palestine, nothing to symbolize the importance of Jerusalem as an Islamic shrine city. It is revealing that in Philip Hitti's book Great Arab Cities, individual chapters are devoted to Mecca, Medina, Damascus, Baghdad, Cairo and Cordova, but none to Jerusalem."
>
> Thomas A. Idinopulos, *Jerusalem*

Jerusalem became significant to Muslims in more than purely religious terms in the twelfth century. Prior to the rise of Islam, the Christians had been the dominant presence in Jerusalem since the time of Constantine in 324 C.E. For centuries, tens of thousands of Christian pilgrims made the journey to Jerusalem and the surrounding area to visit the sites marking the great events in the birth, life, and death of Jesus. To the Christians, it was most disturbing to see Jerusalem and Palestine ruled by the Muslims. In 1095, Pope Urban II decided to take action and launched a holy war with the goal of liberating Palestine from the grip of the Muslims. In 1099, Jerusalem fell to the Crusaders.

To the Muslims, the Christian conquest of Jerusalem was more an insult to their dignity than anything else. The success of the Christian

---

*The religious significance of the Temple Mount to Judaism and Islam is discussed on page 113-116.

armies in Palestine meant that a portion of its territory had fallen into the hands of the infidels. While Jerusalem was no Mecca, Medina, Baghdad, or Cairo, nonetheless, it was an affront to Islam to lose control of the city to a religion that Islam had come to supersede.

A century after the Christian conquest of Palestine, Saladin, a Muslim Kurd, was able to retake Jerusalem for Islam in 1187. His victory came to symbolize the triumph of Islam over the infidels and the maintenance of Islamic integrity throughout the Muslim world. Though the Muslims would again be defeated in Jerusalem by the Crusaders, in 1244 the Christians were driven out for good. For the next seven hundred years, until the defeat of the Ottoman Empire in World War I, Muslims ruled Jerusalem and Palestine. Throughout the centuries of Ottoman rule, Palestine was viewed as a relatively minor extension of Syria and held little value beyond the generation of tax revenues.

Muslim Perspective: Circa 2001

Historically, Islam not only acknowledged the centrality of Israel and Jerusalem to the Jewish people but based its own reverence for Jerusalem on Jewish tradition. As a monotheistic religion, Islam saw itself as the culminating phase of human spiritual development. Mankind's spiritual advance from paganism began with Abraham, Moses, and the Jews; was continued by Jesus; and reached its apex with Muhammad and Islam. This same kind of global spiritual perspective is what underlies Islam's relationship to Jerusalem.

> *"The Dome of the Rock was constructed in 685 over the outcropping of limestone rock which Jewish tradition held to be the place of Abraham's intended sacrifice of Isaac, and the Holy of Holies of Solomon's Temple. In building the Dome of the Rock, the earliest Arab rulers of Palestine expressed their reverence for Jerusalem, city of the prophets... the Dome symbolized both Islam's inheritance from and triumph over Judaism and Christianity."*
>
> Thomas A. Idinopulos, *Jerusalem*

Since the founding of the State of Israel, the historical relationship of Islam to Jerusalem became distorted by the Arab rejection of Israel's right to exist and by militant Islam's goal of reviving a vast Islamic empire. Here, essentially, is how the thinking goes: "Since we view the

State of Israel as an illegitimate foreign entity, we must do all we can to show that the relationship of the Jews to Israel and Jerusalem is tenuous at best and even nonexistent." The result of this position is the widespread embrace of a revisionist, "Jewless" version of the history of Israel and Jerusalem.

In 1979, as part of the Camp David peace accords, the Israelis suggested the creation of a joint Egyptian-Israeli school textbook as a way to "anchor peace in people's minds and hearts." The Egyptians categorically rejected the proposal.

> *"What I saw on the official Egyptian website was mind-boggling. The section on Jerusalem is adorned by a spectacular view of the Dome of the Rock, and five photographs of Israeli soldiers shooting at Palestinian youngsters. These are the only pictures on the website, and they set the tone. The text that follows starts with a simple statement: 'All along human history, Jerusalem has always been an Arab Palestinian city...' Anyone reading this would not imagine that there was ever a historical Jewish presence in Jerusalem or that Jerusalem had any meaning in Judaism—Judaism is not even mentioned. If this is the official Egyptian version, what do those who oppose peace say?"*
>
> Shlomo Avineri, *Jerusalem Post*, December 19, 2000
> Avineri was a member of the delegation
> that negotiated the peace accords with Egypt.

And Now for the Palestinians

The existence of a subgroup of Arab people that possesses a specifically Palestinian identity is a phenomenon that gradually took hold over the course of the last century. For the Arabs of Palestine, when identity went beyond family and village, its next reference point was regional, which meant Syrian. Palestine was traditionally viewed as being the southern part of Syria. The notion of a distinctly Palestinian Arab peoplehood only began to catch on amongst the small, wealthy, elite class in the early-1900s and then trickled down ever so slowly to the masses. The fervor with which Palestinians began to assert their peoplehood in the 1960s and 1970s would have been totally unrecognizable to their grandparents and great-grandparents.

"...During the period from the outset of World War I, the sense of political and national identification of most politically conscious, literate, and urban Palestinians underwent a sequence of major transformations. The end result was a strong and growing national identification with Palestine. In succeeding decades, this identification with Palestine was to be developed and refined significantly, as Palestinian nationalism grew and developed. Equally important, it continued its slow spread beyond the relatively narrow elite which was initially affected by these ideas to broader sectors of the population. So a profound transformation of the sense of self of the Arab population of Palestine, which began during the years immediately before World War I and intensified after it, resulted in the emergence of a Palestinian national identity where a few decades before no such thing had existed."

Professor Rashid Khalidi, *Palestinian Identity: The Construction of Modern National Consciousness*

The rise of nationalism, along with the notion of a people's right to self-determination, resulted in the creation of numerous new independent countries during the twentieth century. When it comes to Palestine and the Palestinians, the question that must be asked is this: If Jordan, Iraq, Lebanon, Bahrain, Syria, and Saudi Arabia are all countries, why isn't Palestine? Or, put another way: Why is it that Yemenite, Lebanese, and Jordanian Arabs all have a country to call their own and Palestinians don't? To this, there are basically three answers: they did, they do, and they will. Let's take a look at each.

They Did—Almost

In the aftermath of World War I and World War II, for the first time in history, the Arab world was subdivided into numerous distinct national entities. Within this process of emerging identities and nation states, one of the proposed new countries was called Palestine, and it was to be populated and governed by the Arabs of Palestine. If this is the case (you are asking yourself), then how come when you look at a map of the Middle East you see Jordan, Lebanon, Israel, and Saudi Arabia but no sign of Palestine? The answer to this question lies in a tragedy that would lead to the needless loss of tens of thousands of lives and the suffering of hundreds of thousands more.

The Arab country of Palestine was scheduled to celebrate its independence from Great Britain in May of 1948, but there was a problem. At the very same time that the country of Palestine was due to come into being, Israel was also due to be born, and therein lay the problem. At the behest of the United Nations, Great Britain had decided that it was going to divide its territory into two new countries, one called Palestine and one called Israel. (See map on p. 153.) The problem was that, while the Jews were prepared to take the reins of sovereignty in Israel (and this was an Israel that did not include Jerusalem, the Gaza Strip, or the West Bank), the Palestinians were not satisfied with their country. The nascent country of Palestine included the entire West Bank and Gaza Strip, as well as much of what today is north and central Israel. Jerusalem was to be a neutral, internationalized city that would reflect its multi-religious identity and would be open to visitors and pilgrims of every faith.

On May 14, 1948, as the British prepared to pull out of the Middle East and as Israel and Palestine sat at the brink of a future of peace and mutually beneficial coexistence, tragedy struck. The Palestinian Arabs, with the full support of their Arab brethren, decided to try and conquer Israel before it could be born and erect a Palestinian state on all of the land vacated by Great Britain.

> *"This will be a war of extermination and a momentous massacre which will be spoken of like the Mongolian massacres and the Crusades."*
> Azzam Pasha, Secretary General of the Arab League, 1948

What transpired as a result of this fateful decision was a war that cost thousands of lives, displaced tens of thousands of families, and in the end resulted in only one new country being born instead of two. Though a fledgling Israel survived the onslaught of six invading armies, Palestine fared much worse. While the Palestinians had anticipated the conquest of Israel, what transpired was their worst nightmare come true. Not only was Israel not vanquished, but all the territory that had been scheduled to form the new homeland was itself conquered—and not just by Israel—but by Egypt and Jordan as well. By the time the war ended in 1949, Jordan was in control of the West Bank, including much of Jerusalem, Egypt was in control of the Gaza Strip, and Israel was in control of the Galilee. The country called Palestine was nowhere to be found. (See map on p. 154.)

From 1949 until 1967, the results of the Arab invasion of Israel defined a new status quo and a new state of being for the Palestinians. Let's take a look at what happened to the Palestinian people who, in 1948, were just one day away from becoming citizens of their own country—a country they are still desperately trying to establish.

Palestinian Refugees: From Where, to Where, and Then What?

As a result of the war of 1948, approximately 700,000 Palestinian Arabs fled their homes.* Due to the failure of the Arab forces to crush Israel, most were unable to return home, and thus were born the Palestinian refugees. Of those Arabs who left their homes, 75,000 were settled in refugee camps in Syria, 100,000 in Lebanon, 70,000 in Jordan, 190,000 in Gaza, and 250,000 in the West Bank. (See map on p. 156.) Another 30,000 of the wealthier Palestinians were able to flee to Europe, Egypt, and elsewhere prior to May 1948. They expected to wait out the war and then return home.

The story of what happened to the Palestinian refugees after 1948 is one of the great human tragedies of the last half of the twentieth century. We will now take a look at that story.

Palestinians of Gaza

The Palestinians of Gaza became a people whose welfare was largely ignored by Egypt and the broader Arab world, and who were thus doomed to a nationally unfulfilled existence on a nonviable bit of the Mediterranean coast. While UN criteria for the settlement of refugee problems would consider Arab countries as natural places for integration, the Egyptian government refused to allow these stateless Arabs to be resettled in Egypt. The people of Gaza were thus cut off both from their Palestinian brethren in the West Bank and elsewhere, as well as from their fellow Arabs in Egypt.

Palestinians of the West Bank and Jerusalem

By war's end, Jordan was in control of East Jerusalem (Israel was in control of the Jewish-populated western portion of the city), the Old City (which included all the Jewish, Christian, and Muslim holy sites),

---

*This figure is based on questionable UN estimates. Israel puts the number at 500,000, while Arabs put it at close to one million.

and the entire West Bank. The Palestinians of these areas fared much better than their fellow nationalists in Gaza. In fact, the Jordanian government viewed the people of Jordan and the people of Palestine as comprising a singular national identity, and thus saw as unnecessary the creation of a separate Palestinian state on the West Bank. In April of 1950, Jordan officially annexed the West Bank and granted Jordanian citizenship to its Palestinian inhabitants. From that point on, the term Palestine was dropped from official usage on all Jordanian documents. In 1953, King Hussein convened the Jordanian Parliament in Jerusalem instead of Amman and announced that from that time forth Jerusalem would function as Jordan's second capital.

Palestinians of Lebanon and Syria

Both Lebanon and Syria kept the great majority of the refugee population confined to refugee camps, where they were cared for by United Nations workers. Those Palestinians who were able to work their way out of the camps and tried to establish more normal lives found that they were often treated as unwanted outsiders in Lebanon and Syria. To this day, Palestinian Arabs are barred from over fifty professions in Lebanon.

Palestinians of Israel and the Galilee

At the end of the war, approximately 150,000 Palestinian Arabs remained in the Galilee and elsewhere in Israel, and, like other Arabs in Israel, they were granted full Israeli citizenship. Today, no official distinction exists amongst the Arabs of Israel—all are citizens, and all have the full benefits of citizenship. Israeli Arabs (including women) vote and organize politically as they like, worship freely and openly, have the largest Arabic free press in the Middle East, and serve as duly elected members of the Israeli Parliament. Ironically, nowhere in the Middle East do Arabs live in as open a society and enjoy such full civil rights as they do in Israel.

Refugees: Yesterday and Today

With 700,000 refugees within their borders, the Arab countries were confronted with a problem that had three potential solutions. One, they could negotiate a comprehensive peace agreement with Israel that would include the creation of a Palestinian state in the West Bank and Gaza capable of absorbing the refugees. Two, they could grant the refugees citizenship, absorb them into their own Arab populations, and give them the opportunity to become full, active, and contributory members of their societies.* Three, they could maintain the refugees in the squalor of the camps where the wounds of their condition would fester, and from where they could aspire to one day successfully launch an effort to undo the catastrophe of '48, and destroy Israel. The Arabs chose door number three.

There is a widespread perception that for fifty years the Palestinian refugees have been suffering under Israeli occupation and have been denied, by Israel, the ability to achieve sovereignty. This, however, simply isn't the case. Until the Six-Day War of 1967, the Palestinians of Jerusalem, the West Bank, and Gaza were living under Arab occupation, not Israeli. For almost twenty years the opportunity existed for the Arab governments to establish a sovereign Palestinian state with Jerusalem as its capital, but they did nothing of the kind.

> *"The insufficiency of the '100,000 offer' [In 1949, Israel reluctantly agreed to take back 100,000 refugees in the context of a comprehensive peace], the Arab states' growing rejectionism, and their inability to publicly agree to absorb and resettle most of the refugees... and America's unwillingness or inability to apply persuasive pressure on Israel and the Arab states to compromise—all meant that the Palestinian exiled Arabs would remain refugees, to be utilized during the following years by the Arab states as a powerful political and propaganda pawn against Israel."*
>
> Benny Morris, *The Birth of the Palestinian Refugee Problem, 1947-1949*

> *"The Arab states do not want to solve the refugee problem. They want to keep it as an open sore, as an affront to the United Nations and as a weapon against Israel. Arab leaders don't give a damn whether the refugees live or die."*
>
> Ralph Galloway, former Director of the UNRWA, 1958

---

*After the war, Arab governments expelled over half-a-million Jews from countries they had lived in for centuries. In the case of Iraq, the Jewish community had been there for over a thousand years. Israel successfully absorbed these Jewish refugees into their newborn country. See map on p. 155.

Welcome to the PLO

As a result of Arab refusal to allow the Palestinians to create a state of their own, Palestinian national aspirations came to be embodied in guerrilla organizations committed to terrorizing Israel and establishing a Palestinian state in "all of Palestine." In 1964, these groups united under the banner of an organization called the PLO—the Palestine Liberation Organization. The PLO was founded with the full support of all Arab governments, had Yasir Arafat as its undisputed leader by 1969, and in 1974 was recognized by the UN as the "sole legitimate representative of the Palestinian people."

> *"Armed struggle is the only way to liberate Palestine. The liberation of Palestine is a national duty to purge the Zionist presence from Palestine. The establishment of Israel is fundamentally null and void... The claim of a historical or spiritual tie between Jews and Palestine does not tally with historical reality...the Jews are not one people with an independent personality. They are rather citizens of the states to which they belong.*
>
> *The Palestinian Arab people rejects every solution that is a substitute for a complete liberation of Palestine... Zionism is a racist and fanatical movement in its formation and fascist and Nazi in its means... Israel is a constant threat to peace in the Middle East and the entire world... The Palestinian Arab people believes in the principles of justice, freedom, sovereignty, self-determination, human dignity and the right of peoples to exercise them."*
>
> Palestinian National Covenant

From its inception in 1964, the PLO was unambiguous about its goal to annihilate Israel. A decade later, with the realization that it was unlikely that Israel would be defeated by one overwhelmingly massive Arab blow, the PLO decided to fine-tune its tactics and officially adopted a "Phased Plan." The core idea of the Phased Plan was to work toward the establishment of a Palestinian state in any part of Palestine possible and then use that as a base from which to eventually conquer all of Israel.

> *"The PLO will struggle by every means, the foremost of which is armed struggle, to liberate Palestinian land and to establish*

the people's national, independent, and fighting government over every part of Palestinian land to be liberated... The Palestinian national authority, after its establishment, will struggle for the unity of the states of confrontation [Egypt, Syria, Lebanon, Jordan, Iraq], to complete the liberation of all the Palestinian land."

Phased Plan, adopted by the
Palestine National Congress in Cairo, 1974

The United Nations, in 1947, had proposed the establishment of two states, one Jewish and one Palestinian. Beyond the creation of new countries, the UN had envisioned a strong economic linkage between the two, such that each would make a dynamic contribution to the development of the other. This in turn would have been a boon for both peoples and for the entire region. Sadly, this vision proved to be, and still remains, just a dream. The irony is that the Palestinian state toward which events at the dawn of the twenty-first century seem to be inching—if and when it is achieved—will be far smaller than what was originally proposed. Additionally, it will be sixty years behind in terms of growth and development and will emerge out of a climate of bitter enmity with its Jewish neighbor, thus severely handicapping the potential for mutually beneficial cooperation. Had the Arab world accepted and aided the development of the Palestinian state in 1948, there is no telling how much death and suffering would have been averted and how different the Middle East would look today. Tragically, a profound historic opportunity was lost, and as a result we continue to watch the grizzly consequences unfold before our eyes on an all-too-regular basis.

They Do—It's Called Jordan

Today it is axiomatic that the Palestinians are a people without a home. While there is no turning back this perception, it doesn't exactly jibe with the history of Palestine.

When most people think of Palestinians, they either think of those Arabs that were displaced by the war of '48, or those who live in the West Bank and Gaza as a people without a homeland. There is, however, another population of Palestinian Arabs that *does* have a country of its own. While almost always discounted in the realm of realpolitik, it is quite informative to remember that Jordan is home to the largest indigenous population of Palestinian Arabs in the world. In fact, before 1921, Jordan was called Palestine. This means that before they became known as Jordanians, the inhabitants of Jordan were called Palestinians. Today, a large percentage of members of the Jordanian Parliament are, in fact, Palestinians.

At this point, you may be either slightly confused or feel like some sort of semantic wool is being pulled over your eyes, but it's not. A quick look at the map on page 152, along with a brief overview of the modern history of Palestine, will reveal that a Palestinian homeland was actually created in 1921 and that it goes by the name of Jordan.

The Palestine Mandate and Jordan

Until World War I, what are today called Lebanon, Syria, Israel, Iraq, and Jordan were all part of the great Ottoman Empire. In 1920, with the defeat of the Turks and the division of the Middle East, the area that today makes up both Israel and Jordan fell to Great Britain in the form of the Palestine Mandate. It is this territory of mandated Palestine that Palestinians look to as a definitive element of Palestinian Arab identity.

> *"Palestine is the homeland of the Palestine Arab people...*
> *Palestine with its boundaries that existed at the time of the*
> *British mandate is an integral regional unit. The Palestinians*
> *are the Arab citizens who were living permanently in Palestine*
> *until 1947, whether they were expelled from there or*
> *remained."*
>
> Palestinian National Covenant, Articles I, II, V

In 1921, in response to political considerations in the Middle East and Europe, Great Britain decided to divide Palestine. Three quarters of Palestine was immediately granted independence, while the status of the remaining quarter hung in abeyance. The portion of Palestine that received independence was named Transjordan (later shortened to Jordan). Thus, in 1921, with the creation of Jordan out of three quarters of Palestine, what took place was the establishment of history's first Palestinian state. The remaining quarter of Palestine would continue under British stewardship until 1948, when it would be divided once again. This second division was intended to be the final one. Had the final division gone as planned, the result would have been that where once a territory called Palestine existed, now there would be three independent states: Jordan, Palestine, and Israel.

Palestinians: The View from Jordan

To Jordan's King Abdullah, there was simply no distinction between the Arabs who lived on the East Bank of the Jordan River—in Jordan—and those who lived on the British-controlled West Bank; all were Palestinians. The Palestinians of Jordan and the Palestinians who lived in what was left of mandated Palestine all shared a common culture, language, and religion.

In 1948, as the second partition of Palestine was moving closer to becoming a reality, King Abdullah had his eye on incorporating the West Bank into Transjordan. Additionally, while a split amongst the Arabs of Palestine existed regarding whether or not they should look to a future that formally linked them to Jordan, in December 1948 a conference of 2,000 Palestinian Arab communal leaders invited King Abdullah to unify Palestine and Jordan.

> *"The king had initially supported the idea of partition, and in this he was motivated by a view that those parts of Palestine allocated to the Arabs should and eventually would be incorporated into neighboring states. Transjordan would take control of the West Bank, the Western Galilee would be added to Lebanon, and Egypt would acquire the Gaza district. Abdullah's attitude toward Palestine was also encouraged by the British, who agreed that Jordanian forces should occupy areas of the country that had been designated for an Arab state."*
> Mark Tessler, A *History of the Israeli-Palestinian Conflict*

Two years after the war, in April 1950, the West Bank, including the major cities of Hebron, Ramallah, Nablus, Jericho, and Bethlehem, as well as most of Jerusalem and all its holy sites, were officially incorporated into Transjordan. All of the Palestinian Arabs living in these areas were granted Jordanian citizenship. A parliamentary resolution that incorporated the West Bank into Jordan formalized "The complete unity between the two sides of the Jordan and their union into one state, which is the Hashemite Kingdom of Jordan." To be sure, there was much debate in the West Bank community regarding whether or not this unification with Jordan represented the fulfillment of its national aspirations or not.

Arafat, the PLO, and Black September

Over the nineteen years from 1948 to 1967, it became clear to Palestinians that if they were to achieve independent sovereignty in all of Palestine, it would only come as a result of their own efforts and not because of the efforts of their fellow Arabs. Egypt had not been willing to give up authority in Gaza, Jordan clearly saw no need for the creation of yet another Arab country, and the grand hope that Israel would be defeated by the surrounding Arab states had been dashed on the rocks of the Six-Day War.

In 1964, the PLO was created to represent the Palestinian cause, take the lead in the ongoing war to liberate Palestine from the Jews, and establish a Palestinian state that might or might not form some kind of formal federation with Jordan. One of the largest of the PLO groups was Al-Fatah. By 1965, Arafat emerged as the leader of Fatah, and its headquarters and primary base of operations were moved to Jordan. Within a few years, Fatah grew to the point where it was becoming a force that could not only harass Israel but also present a threat to the stability of King Hussein's regime as well. Soon, Arafat and the PLO leadership began to think in terms of political autonomy for the Palestinians in Jordan and then beyond that to a fundamental change in the essential character of the country itself. And then came Black September.

By 1969, the PLO presence in Jordan had become so widespread and entrenched that it was functioning as something of a shadow government. The PLO had been granted limited police authority and soon flexed its muscles in ways that directly challenged King Hussein. By September, Arafat had established a centralized Palestinian military command, launched attacks against Jordanian forces, and seized control of an important oil refinery. The Jordanian military itself had a number of officers who were sympathetic to the idea of replacing the Hashemite regime with a Republic of Palestine, and many of its soldiers were poised to defect to the PLO.

On September 17, King Hussein ordered a full-scale attack on the PLO. What followed was two weeks of bloody warfare in the streets of Amman, in Palestinian refugee camps, and elsewhere. In the end, three thousand PLO fighters were dead, and with them died Arafat's aspirations for imposing Palestinian rule on Jordan. Despite the defeat of the PLO and its ouster from Jordan, King Hussein continued to consider himself the rightful guardian of the Palestinian people of the West Bank and Jerusalem, while at the same time Yasir Arafat and the Palestinians continued to view both Israel *and* Jordan as their rightful homeland.

> *"Jordan is ours, Palestine is ours, and we shall build our national entity on the whole of this land."*
> Yasir Arafat, speech at the UN, May 1974

> *"Jordan is Palestine...Jordanians and Palestinians must realize that their fate is the same. Jordan in itself is Palestine."*
> King Hussein, in the Kuwaiti newspaper *Al-Anba*, 1984

They Will—Probably

The future Palestinian state, assuming it doesn't involve the destruction of Israel or a confederation with Jordan, will be made up of almost the entire West Bank and Gaza, a land bridge between the two, and possibly even part of Jerusalem. Since the dramatic Oslo breakthrough in 1993, the Palestinians have been moving closer and closer to their goal of establishing such a state, while Israelis—and indeed Jews the world over—have been moving closer to their dream of not only returning to the land of Israel but of living there in peace.

The next chapter will look at what has transpired over the last decade. As we will see, beginning with the watershed agreement negotiated in Oslo, Norway, events appeared to be moving toward peace in ways that seemed unimaginable for almost half a century. At the same time, a sense of historical déjà vu existed as the Palestinians finally agreed to accept a state of their own, living side-by-side with Israel. What had been proposed by the UN and rejected by the Arabs in 1947, was now being proposed by Israel and accepted in 1993.

Historical Overview Part II

FROM THE OTTOMAN EMPIRE TO THE INTIFADA
The Last Five Hundred years of
Jewish History in the Land of Israel

Rabbi Ovadia Bartinora emigrates to Jerusalem . . . . . 5246/1486 C.E.
Ottoman Empire conquers Syria/Palestine 5277/1517
Sulemain the Magnificent rebuilds Jerusalem walls 5298/1538
Yehuda Hachasid leads 1,000 Polish Jews to Israel 5459/1699
First Aliya; 25,000 Jews emigrate to Israel. 5642/1882
Second Aliya; 30,000 Jews emigrate to Israel 5664/1904
British conquer Palestine 5677/1917
Balfour Declaration. 5677/1917
British mandate for Palestine. 5680/1920
Palestine divided into Transjordan & Palestine 5681/1921
Arabs massacre Jews in Hebron. 5689/1929
UN Partition Plan creates Israel and Palestine 5707/1947
War of Independence; Palestinians & Arabs attack 5708/1948
700,000 Arabs become refugees; Jordan captures
Jerusalem & West Bank; Egypt captures Gaza 1948–1949
600,000 Jews expelled by Arabs & settled in Israel. 1949–1952
Sinai Campaign. 5717/1956
Six-Day War; Israel captures Sinai, Golan Heights,
West Bank, Gaza, Jerusalem and Western Wall 5727/1967
Palestinian terrorists murder Israeli athletes
at Munich olympics 5733/1972
Yom Kippur War. 5734/1973
Terrorists hijack plane; Entebee rescue raid 5736/1976
Egyptian president Anwar Sadat comes to Jerusalem 5737/1977
Israel-Egypt peace accords; Israel returns Sinai 5739/1979
Israel destroys Iraqi nuclear reactor 5741/1981
Lebanon War against PLO 5742/1982
First Intifada; rise of Hamas & Islamic Jihad 1987–1993
40,000 Ethiopian Jews airlifted to Israel 5751/1991
Oslo Accords; PLO recognizes Israel, denounces terror . . 5753/1993
Israel-Jordan peace treaty. 5759/2000
Camp David; Clinton, Arafat & Barak 5759/2000
Al Aksa Intifada; era of Palestinian suicide bombers 5760/2000

peace? from Oslo to *Intifada*

6

On September 9, 1993, after months of intense and secretive negotiations in Oslo, Norway's foreign minister, Johan Jorgan Holst called Yasir Arafat in Tunis to find out, once-and-for-all, if the Palestinians were prepared to accept Israel's right to exist. "Abu Ammar, (Arafat's nom de guerre) *you* must decide. You cannot convene your colleagues now." Finally, Arafat relented and agreed to write a letter to Israeli Prime Minister Yitzchak Rabin. Later that day, Holst flew to Tunis where he picked up the letter and then personally delivered it to Prime Minister Rabin in Jerusalem. Rabin accepted the letter and wrote a short response. Those two letters held out the promise of a future of peace for the land and people of Israel, for the Palestinian Arabs, and for the entire Middle East.

> *Mr. Prime Minister,*
> *I would like to confirm the following PLO commitments:*
> *The PLO recognizes the right of the State of Israel to exist in peace and security.*
> *The PLO commits itself to the Middle East peace process, and to a peaceful resolution of the conflict between the two sides, and declares that all outstanding issues relating to permanent status will be resolved through negotiation.*

The PLO renounces the use of terrorism and other acts of violence and will assume responsibility over all PLO elements and personnel in order to assure their compliance, prevent violations and discipline violators.
Sincerely,
Yasir Arafat, Chairman
The Palestine Liberation Organization
Letter from Yasir Arafat to Prime Minister Yitzchak Rabin, September 9, 1993

Mr. Chairman,
In response to your letter... the Government of Israel has decided to recognize the PLO as the representative of the Palestinian people and commence negotiations with the PLO within the Middle East peace process.
Yitzchak Rabin
Prime Minister of Israel
Letter from Yitzchak Rabin to Yasir Arafat, September 9, 1993

Four days after the exchange of letters between Prime Minister Rabin and Chairman Arafat, a Declaration of Principles was signed on the east lawn of the White House in a dramatic and moving ceremony. The agreement involved a five-year transitional period during which elections would be held for a Palestinian governing council, Israel would withdraw from Gaza and begin a phased withdrawal from the West Bank, and work would begin on the transition of authority from Israel to the Palestinians. The interim period was intended to conclude with permanent status negotiations that would lead to the creation of a Palestinian state living in peace with Israel. It's now nine years since that beautiful fall day on the White House lawn, and once again, the fulfillment of dreams has been delayed.

We will now take a look at the road traveled by the PLO after its defeat in Jordan and see how events led from there to high hopes on the White House lawn and then dashed hopes at Camp David.

Arafat the Terrorist

Over the decade following its defeat in Jordan, the PLO proceeded to re-establish its base of operations in southern Lebanon, where it successfully established a "state within a state." It was within this semi-independent fiefdom in Lebanon that the PLO developed the infrastructure that not only enabled it to plan and launch attacks on Israel but allowed it to become a hub for international terrorism.

> *"The PLO established a territorial base from West Beirut southward. It became the center not only for operations against Israel but for international terrorism as well.*
>
> *During the 1970s, the PLO mini-state in Lebanon functioned as a center for training and arming subversives from the non-communist countries. It was thus largely because of the PLO that the 1970s was a decade of terrorism."*
>
> Jillian Becker, terrorism expert,
> from *Terrorism: How the West Can win*

> *"Terrorism is the cancer of the modern world and dates from the middle 1960s, when the PLO formally adopted terror as its primary policy. Terrorism was thus able to draw on the immense financial resources of the Arab oil states... From 1970 to 1982, the PLO operated a quasi-occupation of Lebanon. It acquired the weaponry of a sizeable modern army and set up terrorist training camps of its own, used as facilities of a score of killer gangs throughout the world."*
>
> Paul Johnson, British historian,
> from *Terrorism: How the West Can Win*

In addition to waging a campaign of murder directed at Israeli civilians and becoming the epicenter for worldwide terrorism, the PLO used its considerable resources in Lebanon to foster the political aspirations of the Palestinians in the West Bank and Gaza. Israel's capture of these territories in the Six-Day War had proven to be a decisive turning point in the Palestinian conflict with Israel. From that point on, and certainly after the PLO expulsion from Jordan, the Palestinians were able to define their cause not only as a struggle to liberate Palestine but also as a struggle to liberate over a million Palestinian Arabs from Israeli rule. This became an extremely effective tactic for achieving international legitimacy for the Palestinian cause. Where once the PLO was perceived as a murderous terrorist organization bent on the annihilation of Israel, it could now present itself in the guise of championing the freedom of a conquered and oppressed people. In reality, Israel never wanted to rule the Palestinians.

Immediately after the war, Israel was prepared to exchange most of what it had captured in exchange for peace. Unfortunately, the Arabs weren't interested in peace and Israel was left with the untenable responsibility of administering a large—and largely hostile—Arab population. In fact, as the years went on, a deep irony emerged out of Israel's stunning victory in the Six-Day War. While the capture of the West Bank provided Israel with desperately needed strategic depth on its western front, this boon in national security came at the price of having to rule a territory populated solely by Arabs. The result was all but inevitable: No matter what kind of social and economic improvements took place under Israeli rule, the Palestinians were always "the occupied" and the Israelis were always "the occupiers," and this inherently antagonistic relationship could only lead to bitter confrontation.

Bye-Bye, Beirut—Hello, Peace Now

By the early 1980s, in addition to being a launching ground for terrorist attacks, the PLO was using southern Lebanon as a base from which to shell Israel's northern cities. In June of 1982, Israel decided that it had to eliminate the PLO's ability to attack it from Lebanon. After invading southern Lebanon, Israel pursued the PLO all the way to Beirut, where it laid siege to the PLO forces positioned throughout the city. By August, Israel had succeeded to the point where an international force was brought into Lebanon to coordinate the evacuation of PLO fighters, their leadership, and Yasir Arafat to Tunis. While the loss of Lebanon was a major blow to the PLO, it wasn't a total loss.

> *"The Lebanese war was the most televised war in history up to that time. The daily television transmission of Israeli artillery bombarding Beirut, the columns of smoke, dust and fire in the air, and the close-up pictures of the destruction, including on one occasion serious damage to a hospital, caused immense harm to Israel's international image, and much anguished discussion in Israel itself."*
>
> Sir Martin Gilbert, *Israel: A History*

Two weeks after the evacuation of the PLO from Lebanon, Israeli troops that were guarding Palestinian refugee camps from rival

Lebanese Christian fighters allowed those forces into two Beirut refugee camps to root out remaining pockets of PLO fighters. What resulted was a massacre that shocked both Israel and the world. By the time it ended, the Lebanese militia had killed and mutilated over two thousand Palestinian men, women and children in the refugee camps of Sabra and Shatilla. Israelis were profoundly disturbed by what had taken place under their watch. A week after the massacre, over 400,000 people (over ten percent of Israel's population), gathered in Tel Aviv to express their outrage.

In Lebanon, while Israel had dealt a decisive blow to terrorism, ironically, for the second time in fifteen years, an Israeli victory would work to enhance the standing of the Palestinian cause. With Israel already in the position of ruling the Arabs of the West Bank and Gaza, and with it now being portrayed as a ruthless invading force in Lebanon, the result was that, in the eyes of the world, the Israeli David had morphed into a brutal Goliath.

As the decade of the eighties progressed, the PLO leadership in Tunis lost much of its influence over the Arabs in the West Bank and Gaza, and its strength and prestige were at an all-time low. At the same time, inside Israel itself more people than ever concluded that Israel's position as an occupying power had become untenable. It wasn't conceivable that Israel could indefinitely control two million Arabs who weren't Israeli citizens, and it was similarly inconceivable that Israel could survive as a Jewish and democratic state if it allowed those same Arabs to become citizens. In the eyes of many, Israel was stuck between a rock and a hard place, and therefore some sort of accommodation with Palestinian nationalism was widely perceived as a vital imperative. It was at this juncture that Israelis themselves became some of the strongest advocates for a Palestinian state. What became known as the Israeli "peace camp" saw no solution to Israel's great existential dilemma other than complete Palestinian sovereignty.

Settlements, Peace, and Security—The Great Debate

Within Israel there raged a great debate: Could Israel survive the existence of a Palestinian state or would it become a mortal danger? Since 1967, the view was that the strategic depth of the West Bank and Gaza were vital to Israel's security. The West Bank's eastern mountains and rugged terrain provided a defensible border as well as an ideal location from which to monitor Arab troop movements. From a military perspective, a hostile Arab state in the West Bank would place the majority of Israel's population only minutes away from the reach of an invading army. Operating from the West Bank, Arab tanks could reach Tel Aviv and cut Israel in half in less than two hours. From Gaza to Israel's coastal cities is just twenty minutes by tank, and enemy planes could be over Jerusalem and Tel Aviv in the blink of an eye. As a small country that relies on mobilizing its civilian reserves in the event of attack, the extra time and space that strategic depth represented could make all the difference in the world. Many were concerned that a Palestinian state, even if it didn't launch any conventional attacks on Israel, would become a base from which terrorists could operate with impunity. It was this kind of thinking that motivated most of Israel's military and political leaders, beginning with Moshe Dayan in 1967, to advocate the establishment of a strong Jewish presence in the West Bank and Gaza. This was the origin of Israel's settlement policy, and the location of Jewish settlements was primarily determined by strategic considerations that would come into play in the event of war. The settlement policy was carried out by every Israeli government since the late sixties, and by the end of the nineties there were approximately 220,000 Jews living in the West Bank and Gaza, 80 percent of whom lived in or near what were basically defensive suburbs around major Israeli cities.

There was and is, however, another point of view. Israeli advocates of a Palestinian state argue that to continue military control of a territory whose population is over 90% Arab is also a threat to Israel's existence. The threat is twofold: First, there is the moral threat—that continued rule of another people is inherently corrupting and compromises the integrity of the Jewish soul. Second, if Israel were to opt for annexation of the West Bank and Gaza and the absorption of the Palestinian Arabs into its citizenry, this would inevitably lead to a binational state whose Jewish identity could be legislated out of existence.

> "Israel stands at a crossroads. The course it chooses will not just affect the tenor of the nation's life but will determine whether it can continue to exist... It is no secret that the crude balance of forces between Israel and the Arabs is evolving in the Arabs' favor [and the] Arabs' ability to absorb losses is ultimately likely to reverse the balance of forces. By annexing the West Bank even only de facto, by continuing to rule it and

build settlements there, Israel increases not only its area but its
Arab population. A Jewish state with an Arab majority, or even
near-majority, is not a viable Jewish state. Ultimately
demography may have a greater influence on the future of the
Arab-Israeli conflict than any other factor."

Yehoshofat Harkabi, *Israel's Fateful Hour.*
Professor Harkabi is a former chief of military intelligence and
one of Israel's leading experts on Arab relations with Israel.

Looking at the situation from this perspective and being confident
that it could persuade the Palestinians to accept a demilitarized country,
the Israeli peace camp was determined to see a Palestinian state come
into existence.

Others, of course, felt that this was playing with fire, a fire that
could threaten to consume all of Israel.

From Intifada to Oslo

Palestinians of the West Bank and Gaza looked on as their leaders
in Tunis lived a life of comfort and were chauffeured around in luxury
automobiles. Arafat and his cohorts were increasingly perceived as being
out of touch and even indifferent to Palestinian realities. With an
absentee leadership, two simultaneous phenomena began to develop in
the territories that would provide the infrastructure for the Intifada, the
Palestinian uprising that eventually led to Oslo. The Arabs of the
territories began to organize themselves as never before. Trade unions
and various organized groups of students, professionals, and
intellectuals coalesced to provide unprecedented structure within
Palestinian society. More importantly, Hamas—a violently militant
Islamic group funded by Iran—built a network of schools, social service
organizations, and mosques that also brought a new sense of
cohesiveness and structure to Palestinian communities. These
institutions also provided Hamas with a platform for disseminating an
Islamic ideology that rejected any kind of peace with Israel.

On December 8, 1987, an Israeli truck driver lost control of his
vehicle on a Gaza road and smashed into a car, killing four Arabs. After
years of bitter confrontation between Israeli soldiers and Arab civilians
and with Palestinian people, towns, and cities organized as never
before, the riots that broke out following this accident proved to be the
spark that ignited the flames of the Intifada. Though the ferocity and

staying power of this popular uprising took both Israel and the PLO leadership by surprise, PLO liaisons in the territories soon managed to take control of events. With time, the Intifada served to rehabilitate Arafat's standing, to further batter Israel's image on the international scene, and to further convince Israelis that finding a way out of their control of the Palestinians was a must. The enduring image of the Intifada became one of stone-throwing Palestinian children confronting heavily armed Israeli soldiers.

> *"The uprising may have achieved its greatest success in the realm of world opinion. In their stone-throwing, barricade-erecting, and tire-burning, the demonstrators very swiftly learned to alert foreign newsmen in advance to ensure broad television coverage of Israeli repression."*
>
> Howard M. Sachar, *A History of Israel*

From Oslo to Camp David

On July 13, 1992, with the Intifada raging into its fifth year, Yitzchak Rabin was sworn in as prime minister of Israel. Rabin was determined not only to end the Intifada but to end the Arab-Israeli conflict. Rabin believed that peace was a dream that was, at long last, within reach.

> *"The new government has accordingly made it a central goal to promote the making of peace and take vigorous steps that will lead to the end of the Arab-Israeli conflict... Within a short time we shall renew the talks in order to diminish the flame of enmity between the Palestinians and the State of Israel. The new government urges the Palestinians in the territories to give peace a chance. We urge the [Palestinian] population, which has been suffering for years, to forswear stones and knives and await the results of the talks that may well bring peace to the Middle East... I invite the King of Jordan, and the Presidents of Syria and Lebanon to this rostrum in Jerusalem, for the purpose of talking peace... for there is no greater victory than the victory of peace. Wars have their victors and their vanquished, but everyone is a victor in peace."*
>
> Yitzchak Rabin, inaugural speech, July 1992

Ten months after Rabin's election, in Oslo, Norway, highly secretive talks began between Israel and the PLO. For the first time ever, Israel was dealing directly with the PLO. Uri Savir, a young director-general in Israel's Foreign Ministry and a protégé of Shimon Peres, departed Israel for Paris on May 20, 1993. The next day, he hung a "please do not disturb" sign on his hotel room door and then left the hotel to catch a flight to Copenhagen—a flight that even his closest aides knew nothing about. From Copenhagen, Savir flew to Oslo where he was met by Terje Larsen, who would serve as his host and introduce him to Abu Ala, the PLO's lead representative and negotiator. When Larsen introduced Savir to Abu Ala he said "Meet your enemy number one, Ahmed Qurei, better known as Abu Ala."

> *"The aim of Israel's elected government is to bring about a historic reconciliation with the Palestinian people. The occupation was forced upon Israel in 1967. Our moral aim is to free ourselves from that condition in a way that will ensure the Palestinians freedom and provide Israel with security... Jerusalem is the center of our national ethos, and if this is open to negotiation, no progress can be made. For our part the stress must be on security, and naturally the PLO will have to cease all terror operations. There is also great potential for economic cooperation and this we must translate into deeds. This is a historic opportunity for us all. It must not be wasted."*
> Uri Savir, opening statement to Abu Ala, May 21, 1993

> *"I would like to convey to your leaders that our intentions— particularly those of our chairman, Yasir Arafat—are serious. We want to live with you in peace. We want to work with you toward developing the region. The situation in the occupied territories is desperate, politically and economically. Time is running out. As for security, I have specific instructions from Arafat to accommodate you on every aspect of this matter."*
> Abu Ala, opening statement to Uri Savir, May 21, 1993

The Oslo talks were taking place against the backdrop of the Intifada, of misery with no end in sight, deadly terrorist attacks, and a creeping sense of despair. Nonetheless, behind the Norwegian veil of secrecy, negotiations progressed slowly but steadily until nine months later when they culminated in a handshake seen around the world.

When, in front of a gallery of dignitaries, Yitzchak Rabin shook the hand of Yasir Arafat on the White House lawn, people were witnessing what only days before had seemed impossible. Yasir Arafat had renounced terrorism, forsworn the aim of Israel's destruction, embraced negotiation as the only means for achieving Palestinian statehood, and extended his hand to the Israeli people. Yitzchak Rabin had embraced the right of the Palestinian people to a country of their own and was prepared to overlook the PLO's terrorist past; have Israel take strategic risks; bet his career, premiership, and legacy on peace; and accept the hand of Yasir Arafat. For the moment, at least, it looked like the Middle East nightmare was drawing to a close.

> *"We who have seen our relatives and friends killed before our eyes, we who have come from a land where parents bury their children, we who have fought against you, the Palestinians— We say to you today in a loud and clear voice: Enough of blood and tears. Enough. We harbour no hatred toward you. We, like you, are people who want to build a home, plant a tree, love, live side by side with you—in dignity, in empathy, as human beings, as free men."*
>
> Yitzchak Rabin, White House ceremony, September 13, 1993

> *"The Government of the State of Israel, and the PLO team representing the Palestinian people, agree that it is time to put an end to decades of confrontation and conflict... and strive to live in peaceful coexistence and mutual dignity and security and achieve a just, lasting and comprehensive peace settlement through the agreed political process..."*
>
> *It is understood that these [permanent status] negotiations shall cover remaining issues, including: Jerusalem, refugees, settlements, security arrangements, borders, relations and cooperation with other neighbors, and other issues of common interest.*
>
> *Disputes arising out of this Declaration of Principles shall be resolved by negotiations."*
>
> From the Oslo Declaration of Principles

As had been anticipated, there were disputes regarding the implementation of peace; nonetheless, it moved forward. By May 1994, Yasir Arafat was the leader of a government-in-waiting—the

Palestinian National Authority. The Palestinian Authority (often referred to as the PA) had legislative as well as judicial powers, was able to negotiate economic agreements with other countries, and had a well-armed police force responsible for internal security. Matters of foreign affairs and defense remained, for the time being, the responsibility of the Israeli government. Additionally, in May of '94, Israel withdrew from Gaza and Jericho, with the result being that almost 900,000 Palestinian Arabs were living under the jurisdiction of the Palestinian Authority.

To say the least, the peace process progressed in a jerky, fit-and-start fashion that at times more resembled conflict than peace. Yet despite crisis after crisis, the process moved forward. By September 1995, the transference of authority from Israel to the PA was underway in the West Bank. While full authority was transferred to the Palestinians in every major West Bank city (representing 29% of the West Bank population) other than Hebron, another 67% of the population lived in areas where, although civil authority was transferred to the PA, internal security was handled jointly by the PA and Israel. This left only 4% of the entire population of the West Bank and Gaza living under Israeli rule.

The road was bumpy, but it continued to point in the direction of a final resolution of the conflict between Israel and the Palestinians. In January 1996, for the first time, Palestinians of the West Bank, Gaza, and East Jerusalem participated in elections to choose their leader as well as eighty-eight members of their governing council. The presence of former U.S. President Jimmy Carter lent great prestige to the oversight of the election process. Yasir Arafat was handily elected to head the PA, at which point President Carter announced that, in essence, what had transpired was nothing less than the birth of the State of Palestine.

When Bumps Became Potholes

While the peace process advanced, many in Israel were having their doubts. The territories under Palestinian control were being used as a base from which brutal terror attacks were launched inside Israel proper, the PA was using the media as well as the classroom to incite continued hatred of Jews and Israel (instead of using them as a means to educate people about peaceful coexistence), and Arafat himself was sending mixed signals about what his true intentions were. Despite all of this, Rabin persisted, driven by the belief that the peace process offered the only realistic alternative to endless death, suffering, and hatred. He knew that many Israelis, as well as many Palestinians were deeply frustrated. Israelis were frustrated by the continuing lack of security and the gnawing sense that they were in fact handing over much of their security to a Palestinian state with suspect intentions. Palestinians were frustrated by the fact that Israel continued building and expanding settlements on the West Bank, by their continued poor economic situation, and by the corruption of the PA leadership.

> *"Arafat continues to run things as a personal fiefdom. There is no freedom of the press under Arafat. But the worst thing, which the elections will not help, is that economically the condition of most Palestinians (especially in Gaza) has deteriorated steadily since Oslo. One of the main reasons for so terrible an economic deterioration is the sheer cost of Arafat's rule through his police force, plus his seven, eight, or nine security apparatuses... at one policeman per fifty people [in Gaza], this is the highest police-per-capita ratio in the world. Arafat spends so much on police he has nothing left to spend on housing, education, health, and welfare."*
> Edward W. Said, *Al-Ahram Weekly* (Cairo), January 18, 1996

On November 4, 1995, the peace process (and indeed the Jewish people) suffered a traumatic loss with the assassination of its greatest advocate, Yitzchak Rabin. Rabin was gunned down at a huge rally for peace by a member of a tiny fringe group opposed to the Oslo peace process. Six months later, Benjamin Netanyahu was elected prime minister on a "peace with security" platform. Netanyahu had been deeply suspicious of the Oslo accords from the outset and was determined to slow down the process and ensure that, if it were to proceed, Arafat and the PA would be closely held to all their commitments.

After three years with Netanyahu at the helm, Israel still had not achieved either peace or security. In May of 1999, Israel elected a new prime minister who seemed to be the perfect man for the job. As the most decorated soldier in the history of the Israeli Defense Forces, Ehud Barak had impeccable credentials as a man who understood what it would take to achieve security. As a close protégé of Yitzchak Rabin, he was committed to the vision of the Oslo accords. If ever there was someone who could carry out the Rabin mandate, it was Ehud Barak.

Let's Call It a Day and Go Home

In 1979, at the Camp David retreat in the Maryland countryside, President Carter had convened a historic summit at which he, Egyptian President Anwar Sadat, and Prime Minister Menachem Begin hammered out the Camp David peace accords between Israel and Egypt. Twenty years later, in the summer of 2000, President Clinton convened a summit, once again at Camp David, where he, Ehud Barak, and Yasir Arafat were to resolve all the outstanding issues and finally achieve the peace that had been the promise of Oslo.

September 13 had been set as the deadline for a final peace agreement leading to the creation of a Palestinian state, and to President Clinton it appeared that the situation had reached the "now or never" point. Both Barak and Arafat would have to face the moment of truth and make the hardest decisions of their lives for the sake of achieving a just and lasting peace. The core issues that would have to be resolved if Camp David were to succeed were the final borders of the Palestinian state, the status of Jerusalem, the "right-of-return" for Palestinian refugees, and the status of Jewish settlements in the West Bank and Gaza.

Both Ehud Barak and Yasir Arafat came to Camp David knowing that the terms of a final settlement were going to leave significant portions of their respective people unhappy. In Israel, some feared that Barak was prepared to relinquish too many strategic assets in the West Bank, that he would abandon most of the settlements, or that he would consent to some kind of division of Jerusalem and the establishment of a Palestinian capital there. On the Palestinian side, many, including the followers of Hamas and Islamic Jihad were against any kind of settlement at all and were prepared to take up arms against Arafat and the PA if he were to sign a deal. There were also those who feared that Arafat would settle for less than the dismantling of 100 percent of the settlements and go soft on the Palestinian "right of return." The right of return is the claim that even if a Palestinian state is created, still, any Palestinians wanting to return to their original places of residence inside Israel itself should be allowed to do so.

For his part, President Clinton was prepared to essentially clear his schedule of everything else, and pitch his tent at Camp David for as long as it would take to get the two leaders to make the kinds of compromises that would be necessary to achieve peace.

Things didn't go exactly as President Clinton had hoped.

So Close and Yet So Far

On July 10, 2000, three smiling faces were at the front door of the Laurel cabin on the grounds of Camp David. A smiling President Clinton was holding the door open to welcome his guests, and Ehud Barak was playfully pushing Yasir Arafat through the door and toward the President. That was probably the last time the three of them smiled together, because at Camp David everything unraveled.

Ehud Barak came to Camp David prepared to make compromises beyond anything Israel had ever considered and perhaps even beyond what large segments of the Israeli people were prepared to endorse. Nonetheless, Barak was convinced that, if Arafat agreed to sign a peace agreement, it would be impossible for Israel to turn its back on a moment of unique historical potential. To achieve his goal of two states living side-by-side in peace, Barak put a bold plan on the table. His proposal included Israeli withdrawal from over ninety percent of the West Bank and Gaza, the uprooting of thousands of Jewish settlers, the relinquishing of a strategic presence along the Jordan, the establishment of a Palestinian state with a presence in Jerusalem, control over the Temple Mount, and a symbolic return of 40,000 refugees along with internationally-backed financial compensation for hundreds of thousands of others. What Barak was not prepared to accept was the relinquishing of Jewish sovereignty over the majority of Jerusalem—including the Old City, the Jewish Quarter, and the Western Wall—and the right of hundreds of thousands of Palestinians to flood the State of Israel. To accept the principle of the right of return would be suicide for the Jewish state, and that neither Barak nor any Israeli was prepared to consider.

Arafat balked. Try as they might, neither Ehud Barak nor President Clinton could get Yasir Arafat to budge. Not only did he reject Israel's proposals, but surprisingly, he didn't offer any counter-proposals of his own. Arafat wanted more of Jerusalem than he knew any Israeli leader could accept, insisted on the full right of return, and refused to sign a deal that would finally end the Israeli-Palestinian conflict. On Tuesday, July 25, after two grueling weeks at Camp David, President Clinton announced that his efforts at achieving peace had come up short. The question immediately became: Where do we go from here?

The Palestinians had already announced that on September 13— peace or no peace—they were going to unilaterally declare the statehood of Palestine. As the talks broke up, the specter of violence suddenly seemed far closer than the promise of peace.

> *"The Government of Israel, and I as Prime Minister, acted out of moral and personal commitment, and supreme national obligation to do everything possible to bring about an end to the conflict... we touched the most sensitive nerves, ours and the Palestinians, but regretfully, with no result. Yet, if we will find ourselves in a confrontation, we will be able to look straight into the eyes of our children and say that we have done everything to prevent it. Israel was prepared to pay a painful price to bring about an end to the conflict, but not any price. Arafat was afraid to make the historic decisions necessary at this time in order to bring about an end to the conflict. The vision of peace is not dead, but it suffered a heavy blow because of the Palestinian stubbornness."*
>
> Ehud Barak, July 25, 2000

> *"After fourteen days of intensive negotiations between Israelis and Palestinians, I have concluded with regret that they will not be able to reach an agreement at this time. Prime Minister Barak showed particular courage, vision and an understanding of the historical importance of the moment. Chairman Arafat made it clear that he, too, remains committed to the path of peace. Now the two parties must go home and reflect, both on what happened at Camp David and on what did not happen."*
>
> President Clinton, July 25, 2000

> *"Prospects of peace have never been stronger in the wake of the Camp David Summit. The gaps are still there, but the summit has laid the foundation for achieving a comprehensive peace between Israelis and Palestinians... We will agree to a deal only if Jerusalem is the capital of both a Palestinian state and Israel."*
>
> Saeb Erakat, July 25, 2000

> *"Mr. Arafat will return home to a hero's welcome, not just in the West Bank and Gaza Strip but in the Arab world."*
>
> Hani al-Hassan, a central committee member of Mr. Arafat's Fatah movement, quoted in *The New York Times*, July 26, 2000

(Chairman Arafat made no personal remarks at the conclusion of Camp David. Remarks were left to his aides and members of his negotiating team.)

Reflections on Camp David

The failure of the Camp David talks was a turning point for Israel and for the Jewish people. In the first half of the twentieth century, two events took place that forever changed the course of Jewish history and the dynamics of Jewish life everywhere. These two events were the Holocaust and the large-scale return of the Jewish people to the land of Israel, culminating in the founding of the State of Israel. In the second half of the century, in a way that hadn't been true for two thousand years, Israel became a central, if not the central, element in the lives of Jews around the world. From the moment of its birth in 1948, Israel had struggled on two fronts—one internal and one external. On the internal home front, Israel had struggled to build a vibrant, open democracy, a thriving economy, and a country that could provide a safe haven for Jews from places like the Soviet Union, Iraq, Egypt, Argentina, Ethiopia, and elsewhere. In many ways, it had succeeded beyond anyone's wildest expectations. Also on the home front, Israeli culture became a focal point for Jewish culture, and—for the first time since the early Talmudic period—Israel became home to the most prominent *yeshivot* (academies of traditional Jewish study) in the world and the center of Jewish religious life. At the heart of it all was a dream—the dream that the Jewish people would be able to live in peace in their ancient homeland. For the first forty-five years of Israel's existence, the dream seemed to be just that—a dream, a dim and distant hope.

For decades, Israel also waged an external struggle, as it fought for survival against a host of enemies sworn to its destruction. None were more implacable than Yasir Arafat and the Palestinians.

Then, in 1993, everything appeared to change. Rabin and Arafat shook hands, negotiations replaced deadly confrontation, and the dream seemed about to come true. With the failure at Camp David, and the outbreak of the Intifada seven weeks later, the dream came crashing back to earth.

The following are some reflections on Camp David more than a year after it took place.

> "*They offered us less than a bantustan, for your information. They have control of the Jordan Valley, with five early warning stations there. They have to control the air above, the water aquifers below, the sea and the borders. They have to divide the*

West Bank in three cantons. No sovereignty over Haram al-Sharif. And refugees, we didn't have a serious discussion."

Yasir Arafat, July 2001

"At Camp David, Mr. Arafat well understood that the moment of truth had come and that painful decisions needed to be made by both sides. He failed this challenge. The assertion now made by some observers that Mr. Arafat was pushed unwillingly to make peace at Camp David is somewhat strange. He signed a series of agreements committing him to make peace in 1993. He even received a Nobel Peace Prize to encourage him to live up to his commitments. At some point in the future a new Palestinian leadership will emerge, capable of making the decisions that would make peace with Israel possible. When this time comes, I am confident that the contours of the agreement will resemble the sound ideas discussed at Camp David."

Ehud Barak, July 2001

"I was at Camp David and I, too, was frustrated almost to the point of despair by the Palestinians' passivity and inability to seize the moment. But there is no purpose—and considerable harm—in adding to their real mistakes a list of fictional ones. Yes, what was put on the table was more far-reaching than anything any Israeli leader had discussed in the past. But it was not the dream offer it has been made out to be, at least not from a Palestinian perspective. Israel was to annex nine percent of the West Bank; in exchange, the new Palestinian state would be granted sovereignty over parts of Israel proper, equivalent to one-ninth of the annexed land. In Jerusalem, Palestine would have been given sovereignty over many Arab neighborhoods of the eastern half and over the Muslim and Christian quarters of the Old City. While it would enjoy custody over the Haram al-Sharif, the location of the third holiest Muslim shrine, Israel would exercise overall sovereignty over this area, known to Jews as the Temple Mount. This too, was far more than had been thinkable only a few weeks earlier, and a very difficult position for the Israeli people to accept. But how could Mr. Arafat have justified to his people that Israel would retain sovereignty over some Arab neighborhoods, let alone the

Haram al-Sharif? Finally, Camp David was not rushed. By the spring of 2000, every serious Israeli, Palestinian, and American analyst was predicting an outbreak of Palestinian violence absent a major breakthrough in the peace process."

Robert Malley, Special Assistant for Arab-Israeli Affairs
to President Clinton, *The New York Times*, July 8, 2001

"It is not just that he [Arafat] had, in the words of President Clinton, 'been here fourteen days and said no to everything.' All he did was repeat old mythologies and invent new ones, like, the Temple was not in Jerusalem. At no point did Chairman Arafat demonstrate any capability to conclude a permanent status deal. Because it requires personal redefinition and giving up myths, I simply do not believe he is capable of doing a deal."

Ambassador Dennis B. Ross, Special Middle East
Coordinator under President Clinton,
New York Review of Books, September 20, 2001,

"For me this was the test: if they insisted on the right of return, that would be conclusive evidence that there could be no end to the conflict. It would mean that it was not their achievement of self-determination that would end the conflict, but their destroying our self-determination. They said we should first deal with the 375,000 refugees in Lebanon... one of them said, 'You will hardly notice them.'"

Dan Meridor, Member of Camp David
Israeli negotiating team, July, 2001

"The Palestinian perspective was that Oslo was a compromise and that it was the last compromise. We were not aware of this. We all thought that somewhere down the road there would be another compromise, which would then be final."

Shlomo Ben-Ami, July 2001.
Ben-Ami was Israeli Foreign Minister and
a senior Oslo and Camp David negotiator.

"Arafat turned away from what was offered and headed straight back into his people's familiar history: the maximalism, the inability to read what can and cannot be had in a world of

nations. He would again let play on his people the old dream that they could have it all, from the river to the sea. He must know better, it is reasonable to presume. But there still lurks in the Palestinian and Arab imagination a view, depicted by the Moroccan historian Abdallah Laroui, that "on a certain day, everything would be obliterated and instantaneously reconstructed and the new inhabitants would leave, as if by magic, the land they had despoiled." Arafat knew the power of this redemptive idea... better the fire of an insurrection than the risks of reconciling his people to a peace he had not prepared them for: this is Arafat's way. This is why he spurned the offer at Camp David in the summer of 2000."

Fouad Ajami, *Foreign Affairs*, November/December 2001
Fouad Ajami is the Majid Khadduri Professor
and Director of Middle East Studies at Johns Hopkins University.

"[Mr. Arafat] showed himself at Camp David, and after, as a man who would rather get nothing for his people than look them in the eye and say, 'We're going to get some things and not others.'"

Thomas L. Friedman, *New York Times*, August 7, 2001
Mr. Friedman is a strong supporter of the Oslo accords,
and author of *From Beirut to Jerusalem*.

Welcome to the Temple Mount

Seven weeks after the conclusion of the Camp David talks, the Palestinians launched a violent uprising that came to be known as the Al Aksa Intifada. Before looking at the Intifada and its impact on Israel and the Oslo peace process, we will take a look at the Temple Mount and its place in Judaism and Islam.

Before, during, and after Camp David, perhaps the most prominent of all the core issues was Jerusalem—and Jerusalem is an issue with a core of its own. At the heart of Jerusalem is the Temple Mount, the plateau designated by Judaism as the site for the holy Temple. For the Jewish people, the Temple Mount in Jerusalem is the holy place par excellence. Though the First and Second Temples were destroyed and though later Muslim conquerors built mosques where they once stood, in Jewish law the spiritual sanctity of the Mount is eternal. In Judaism, there is no other place whose sanctity and significance compares to the Temple Mount. Today, all that remains of the Temple is the outer retaining wall of the Temple Mount, known as the Western Wall. Since this is all that remains, the Western Wall has served as the focal point of Jewish prayer, hope, and aspiration throughout the centuries. As we mentioned before, wherever synagogues are built around the world, they are built facing Jerusalem. Similarly, synagogues in Jerusalem are built facing the Temple Mount. In terms of the temporal world, for the Jewish heart and soul there is only one destination—Jerusalem and the Temple Mount.

In Islam, Jerusalem and the Temple Mount also have significance, though they pale in comparison to Mecca and Medina. Nonetheless, over time, the Al Aksa Mosque and the great golden dome that caps the Dome of the Rock became classified as the third holiest site in Islam.

The Al Aksa Mosque dates back to the year 637 C.E., when Caliph Omar, who had been a personal associate of Muhammad, conquered Jerusalem. After conquering Jerusalem, Omar wanted to see the site of Solomon's great Temple. He also wanted to establish a mosque in Jerusalem that would not clash with established churches and Christian shrines. Because of his regard for the site of the Jewish Temple and because Christians had used it as a garbage dump, Omar decided to have the area cleared and to build his mosque there. Omar's spiritual regard for the Temple Mount was a direct result of its having been holy to the Jews.

> "It came naturally to the Muslims to consult the Jews about the disposition of the site that had been sacred to their ancestors. The distinguished tenth-century historian Abu Jafar al-Tabari says that, 'Omar began his meeting with Kaab [a learned Jew who was consulted about the Temple Mount] by reciting Surahs 17 and 18 of the Koran, which tell the stories of David, Solomon and the Temple.'"
>
> Karen Armstrong, *Jerusalem: One City, Three Faiths*

The Dome of the Rock was first built about half a century after the Muslim conquest of Jerusalem. Unlike Al Aksa, the Dome of the Rock is a shrine and not a mosque. Rather than a place of prayer, it is a place of contemplation. The inside is adorned with verses taken from Islamic texts.

Today it is common to hear about the Dome of the Rock as having been built on the site of the "furthest mosque." This mosque is a central element in Mohammed's "night journey" to heaven, a journey described in the Koran (17:1) as follows, "Glory be He who took his Servant by night from the Sacred Mosque to the Furthest Mosque."

> "It [the Night Journey] was not intended to be taken literally: the early sources make it clear that this was a mystical event in the Prophet's life."
>
> Karen Armstrong, from *How Did This Happen?*

Though the "Sacred Mosque" of the Night Journey is clearly a reference to Mecca, the meaning of the "Furthest Mosque" is highly ambiguous. One problem in linking the Furthest Mosque with Jerusalem is that at the time of the recording of the night journey in the Koran—around the year 621—Jerusalem had yet to be conquered by the Muslims and there simply were no mosques in the city at the time.

> "Muhammad ibn al-Hanafiya (638-700), a close relative of the Prophet Muhammad, is quoted as denigrating the notion that the prophet ever set foot on the Rock in Jerusalem. [The Umayyads] 'pretend that God put His foot on the Rock in Jerusalem, though only one person ever put his foot on the rock, namely Abraham.'"
>
> Daniel Pipes, *Middle East Quarterly*, Fall 2001

> "All subsequent holy places in the Islamic world derive their holiness from Mecca... [Caliph] Abd al-Malik's greatest contribution to the city [Jerusalem] was undoubtedly the Dome of the Rock. Later Muslims would believe that Muhammad had ascended to heaven from the rock after his Night Journey. But in 688 this event had not yet been definitely linked with Jerusalem: had Abd al-Malik intended to commemorate the Night Journey, he would certainly have inscribed the appropriate Koranic verses somewhere in the shrine. But he did not do so."
>
> Karen Armstrong, *Jerusalem: One City, Three Faiths*

The matter of Jerusalem, and the Temple Mount in particular, was always the most sensitive of all the issues that had to be resolved before a final agreement could be achieved. Since 1967, when Israel captured the Old City and the Temple Mount, Israel made sure to respect Muslim sensitivities regarding their holy sites and left matters of practical day-to-day administration of the Mount in the hands of Muslim religious authorities. The first law passed by the Knesset following the Six-Day War, the Protection of Holy Places Law, guarantees freedom of access to all of Jerusalem's holy sites. Jews everywhere, despite their unique relationship to the Temple Mount, were always prepared to accommodate the religious needs of Muslims and fully expected that the Arabs would be granted some kind of special status on the Mount. Unfortunately Muslims, and Palestinians in particular, have been reluctant to show the same kind of deference to Judaism and its relationship to Jerusalem and the Temple Mount. In fact, since the Oslo accords, an ongoing campaign has been waged in the Palestinian press, and through sermons in mosques throughout the West Bank and Gaza, to deny any Jewish claim to its most venerated site. Even at Camp David, it was reported that President Clinton was angered by Palestinian denials of Jewish history.

> *"At the height of a debate hosted by President Clinton on the status of the Temple Mount, shortly before the summit broke down, Sa'eb Erekat, a senior Palestinian negotiator, reportedly asked Shlomo Ben-Ami, 'How do you know that your holy Temple was located there?' The Palestinian Authority's Planning Ministry website, in its sections on history and on Jerusalem, makes no mention of Jews, Judaism, the Bible or the Temple. The site details only the significance of the city for Muslims and Christians. The Israeli Tourism Ministry website, by contrast, highlights the city's significance to Jews, Christians, and Muslims, and identifies Al-Aksa mosque as Islam's third holiest shrine."*
>
> Jerusalem Report, September 11, 2000

> *"There is not even the smallest indication of the existence of a Jewish Temple on this place in the past. In the whole city [of Jerusalem], there is not even a single stone indicating Jewish history. Our right, on the other hand, is very clear." [Die Welt interviewer: "It is agreed among archaeologists that the Wailing Wall is part of the foundation of Herod's Temple. The Bible and other antique sources report about this place in detail. Why can't you respect the Jewish connection to the*

place?"] "It is the art of the Jews to deceive the world. But they can't do it to us. There is not a single stone in the Wailing Wall relating to Jewish history. The Jews cannot legitimately claim this wall, neither religiously, nor historically."

Ikrima Sabri, the PA Mufti, the chief Palestinian religious leader appointed by Arafat, from an interview in the German magazine *Die Welt*, January 2001

Intifada II: Everybody's Invited

The essence of Oslo was that the Palestinians had committed to settling all disputes—and to achieving a Palestinian state—at the negotiating table. Following Camp David, Yasir Arafat concluded that, while Israel could only go so far at the bargaining table, perhaps if he unleashed terror on Israeli civilians, that would create the kind of public pressure that would lead to more concessions being offered in exchange for the tranquility of peace. This tactical decision made a mockery of the Oslo accords.

"Violence is near and the Palestinian people are willing to sacrifice even 5,000 casualties."

Freih Abu Meddein, PA Minister of Justice, August 24, 2000, in the official PA newspaper *Al-Hayut al-Jadida*

"We will advance and declare a general Intifada for Jerusalem. The time for the Intifada has arrived."

PA publication *Al-Sabah*, September 11, 2000

"Speaking at a symposium in Gaza, Palestinian Minister of Communications, Imad Al-Falouji, confirmed that the Palestinian Authority had begun preparations for the outbreak of the current Intifada from the moment the Camp David talks concluded, this in accordance with instructions given by Chairman Arafat himself. Mr. Falouji went on to state that Arafat launched this Intifada as a culminating stage to the immutable Palestinian stance in the negotiations, and was not meant merely as a protest to Israeli opposition leader Ariel Sharon's visit to the Temple Mount."

Al-Ayyam (Palestinian daily newspaper), December 6, 2000

On September 28, 2000, with Arafat threatening to unilaterally declare a state with Jerusalem as its capital—and with Arafat also claiming that the Temple Mount was occupied territory—Ariel Sharon decided to make a symbolic visit to the Temple Mount. Sharon sought and received permission for his visit from the PA and it took place two days before Rosh Hashanah. By the time Yom Kippur and Sukkot were over three weeks later, the Al Aksa Intifada was a murderous, gruesome reality.

In the immediate aftermath of the outbreak of violence, Sharon's visit was often portrayed as the cause of the Intifada. However, a U.S. investigation led by former senator George Mitchell confirmed what Palestinians themselves had already acknowledged:

> *"Although Israelis viewed the visit in an internal political context, Palestinians saw it as highly provocative. From the perspective of the PLO, Israel responded to disturbances with excessive and illegal use of deadly force against demonstrators. From the perspective of the Government of Israel, the demonstrations were organized and directed by the Palestinian leadership to create sympathy for their cause around the world. For Israelis, the lynching of two military reservists in Ramallah on October 12 reflected a deep-seated hatred of Israel and Jews. The Sharon visit did not cause the Al-Aksa Intifada. But it was poorly timed."*
>
> Mitchell Report, May 20, 2001

> *"If this new cycle of warfare pits Sharon against Arafat, that is exactly the kind of war and adversary that Arafat called forth. With brutal efficiency, it was his launching of the war in September 2000—upon his return from Camp David and his spurning of the peace offered him—that resurrected Sharon's political career. As a gambler and adventurer averse to the normal work of nations, Arafat made peace with Israel only to break it."*
>
> Fouad Ajami, *U.S. News & World Report*, April 8, 2002

On the ground in Israel, it was eminently clear that not only was the new Intifada not spontaneous, but it also belied a deeper reality. The speed and ferocity of the Intifada revealed a Palestinian society that professed a readiness to live in peace with Israel but that in fact was seething with hatred. To Israelis, the Intifada said: the core issue in the Middle East is not a Palestinian state that doesn't exist, but a Jewish state that does.

The following are respected and influential voices from within the Israeli peace camp. These are the voices of people who for years worked for peace and were staunch advocates of the Oslo peace process. The Al Aksa Intifada dramatically affected their thinking.

"I had countless meetings with Palestinians. I had more meetings with Palestinians than Shimon Peres or Yossi Beilin did. During all of my meetings with them, they said that we will find a mutually accepted formula for peace. The truth is, this was all a lie ...It became clear to me that the speeches made by Nabil Sha'ath—the same person who was my best friend in America and who came to hug me and kiss me following my pro-peace speeches—were worthless. He did not mean anything he said... After the disco massacre of the Israeli teenagers, when I saw the Palestinians on television dancing in the streets of the West Bank celebrating the slaughter of Israeli teenagers, I was in total disbelief. To a certain degree, we wished for peace so much that we ended up turning our wishes into factual reality. However, there is not going to be peace, not next year and not five years from now. I am not abandoning the path of peace. However, I also refuse to abandon my people and my right to live."

Chaim Shur, June 2001. Chaim Shur is a highly regarded Israeli intellectual. As editor of *The New Outlook* in the '80s, he was one of the first to call for the creation of a Palestinian state.

"Jerusalem has been burning... For many years, we in Israel's peace camp never gave up on peace. We talked to the Palestinians in times when it was not popular in Israel, in times of trauma, animosity and hostility. Now, at the home stretch of long, drawn-out and heated negotiations over a lasting peace agreement, we who advocated peace are facing an enormous crisis of confidence. The events of the last couple of days make us ask ourselves: Do we really understand what is going on? After everything was given, there are still demands on the other side. Suddenly we discovered that what we mean by peace— which is mutual reconciliation—is not being met by the other

side in the same spirit."

Avraham Burg, *New York Times* October 4, 2000

Avraham Burg is speaker of the Knesset and Labor party leader.

"In retrospect it turned out that for Arafat it [Oslo] was a huge camouflage net behind which he fomented, and continues to foment, political pressure and terrorism in different dosages in order to undermine the very idea of two states for two nations."

Shlomo Ben-Ami, October 21, 2001

Ben-Ami was Barak's lead negotiator at Camp David.

"When Arafat rejected the Clinton plan, turned the right of return into a matter of principle, and denied that Israel has any right at all to the Temple Mount, it became clear that the Palestinians were not prepared for a historical compromise. Whoever expected Yasir Arafat to turn into Nelson Mandela was proved wrong, but admitting it is hard. Incredibly hard. When the other side cannot come up with a single intellectual prepared to state clearly, without mumbling, that the murder of children in a pizzeria is a crime, then the Israeli left has no ally. Whoever sees the cold-blooded murder of children and the establishment of settlements as belonging to the same moral category has himself lost all sense of morality."

Shlomo Avineri, *Ha'aretz*, August 24, 2001

Avineri is a leading Israeli intellectual, professor of political science and visiting scholar at the Carnegie Endowment for International Peace. He has been calling for direct negotiations with the PLO and a two-state solution since 1970.

"I have one clear conclusion from the madness of the past few weeks. No matter what the future holds, be it war or peace, at the end of the day what is needed is a separation between them and us. Israel on one side of the border. Palestine on the other. Divorce, not marriage."

Hirsch Goodman, founding editor of
The Jerusalem Report and strong Oslo advocate, November 6, 2000

Palestinian atrocities carried out during the Intifada shocked and horrified Israelis. This was the wolf in sheep's clothing writ larger than life—and the writing was in blood. Teenagers waiting in line at a disco were blown to pieces by a bomb packed with screws and nails. After a mob literally tore two Israelis to pieces, a jubilant murderer triumphantly waved his bloody hands to the glee of the crowd. Two teenage boys who had skipped school and were playing not far from home were so viciously pummeled to death that it was difficult to identify their bodies.

A Palestinian sharpshooter put a bullet through an infant's head. An attack on a school bus left three siblings without limbs and other children dead and wounded. Among the many victims of a pizza shop massacre were a couple and three of their five children. A beloved mother and teacher died in a hail of bullets on her way to school. A wheelchair-bound teenager was having dinner at an outdoor café with a friend. Now they are both in wheelchairs, their bodies ravaged by flying shrapnel. A bat mitzvah celebration became hell-on-earth when a Palestinian burst into the party hall and opened fire on the bat mitzvah girl's friends and relatives. Hundreds and hundreds of families were shattered in sudden, brutal and, irreparable ways.

> *"Families decimated. Celebration turned to horror. Resilience tested again far beyond all reasonable limits. Our critics and our enemies, Yasir Arafat included, would have us believe that this is our fault, that we bring disaster on ourselves: in general, through our refusal to compromise; in particular, through the Sharon Government's ongoing policy of targeted killings. Forgive the repetition, but I will write this over and over for as long as the false accusations are leveled: The overwhelming majority of Israelis have demonstrated at the ballot box their desire to negotiate a territorial settlement with the Palestinians, and have been rebuffed by Arafat, who remains committed to policies that would spell the end of the Jewish state."*
> David Horowitz, editor, *The Jerusalem Report*, February 11, 2002

The collapse of the Oslo peace process and the barbaric viciousness of the Intifada can be traced to two seminal factors. One is Arafat's hidden agenda and the other is Hamas's explicit agenda.

If You Liked Arafat, You Will Love Hamas

By the late '80s, large portions of the Palestinian population had come to embrace Hamas, the Islamic Resistance Movement. Hamas is an Islamic movement whose influence in Palestinian affairs eventually grew to rival that of Yasir Arafat and the Palestinian Authority. Hamas harbors no hidden agendas. Its aim is to cleanse the Arab world of all foreign, non-Muslim influences. At the top of its list in the campaign to restore Islam to its former glory is the need to destroy Israel.

> *"The Movement's program is Islam. From it, it draws its ideas, ways of thinking and understanding of the universe, life and man... It strives to raise the banner of Allah over all of Palestine. In the absence of Islam, strife will be rife, oppression spreads, evil prevails and schisms and wars will break out ...Initiatives, and so-called peaceful solutions [in Palestine] and international conferences, are in contradiction to the principles of the Islamic Resistance Movement. In the face of the Jews' usurpation of Palestine, it is compulsory that the banner of Jihad be raised. The day that the Palestine Liberation Organization (PLO) adopts Islam as its way of life, we will become its soldiers, and fuel for its fire that will burn the enemies."*
>
> The Hamas Covenant, August 1988

A significant cultural divide exists between liberal democratic societies in the West and Arab societies of the Middle East that are totalitarian and Islamic, some of them radically so. Because of this divide, it is very difficult for the Western mind to grasp how profoundly influential a strict and militant form of Islam has become to hundreds of millions of Arabs, especially since the successful Islamic revolution in Iran led by Ayatollah Khomeini in 1979. To people in the West, the outlooks and ideologies expressed by Islamic leaders often seem to be otherworldly. It's as if the pronouncements made in the name of Islam emanate from a vanished world, and so the Western mind says to itself, "They can't really be serious."

> *"The veiled commander stood up, a Hamas flag in one hand and a Koran in the other. The crowd roared Allahu akhbar! (Allah is great!) The Hamas commander spoke: 'Greetings from the occupied land.' He gave a report describing in methodical detail Hamas terrorist attacks, reveling in the bloody results of each attack. The date: 1989. The location: Kansas City. The commander was addressing and thanking the*

Islamic Association for Palestine and the Occupied Land Fund, two organizations holding a conference in the country they called home.

In December 1992, I wandered inside [the Oklahoma City Convention Center] and found books preaching Islamic Jihad, books calling for the extermination of Jews and Christians, even coloring books instructing children on subjects such as 'How to Kill the Infidel.' It was a meeting of the Muslim Arab Youth Association. I was horrified to witness a long procession of speakers, including the head of Hamas, Khalid Misha'al, taking turns preaching violence and urging the assembly to use Jihad against the Jews and the West. At times spontaneous shouts of 'Kill the Jews' and 'Destroy the West' could be distinctly heard.

I attended a five-day Muslim conference in Detroit in December 1993. This annual gathering featured speakers and representatives from some of the world's most militant fundamentalist organizations, including Hamas."

Steven Emerson, *American Jihad*

The Jews of Israel have known for decades how deadly serious these people truly are. Tragically, on September 11, 2001, the rest of the world also learned—through an event that seemed otherworldly—just how serious one has to take an enemy driven by militant Islamic principles.

"Our belief is that this war, between us and the Jews, will continue to escalate until we vanquish the Jews and enter Jerusalem as conquerors. We are not merely expecting a Palestinian state with Jerusalem as its capital; we are heralding the creation of an Islamic caliphate with Jerusalem as its capital. Oh beloved of Allah, as we always say: When the battles between the Muslims and the infidels begin, the martyrs and the slain Muslims will reach paradise."

Sheikh Ibrahim Madhi, September 21, 2001
From the weekly sermon at the Ijlin mosque in Gaza,
which the Palestinian Authority televises every week.

"The willingness for sacrifice and for death we see amongst those who were cast by Allah into a war with the Jews, should not come at all as a surprise...the martyr, if he meets Allah, is

forgiven with the first drop of blood; he is saved from the torments of the grave; he sees his place in paradise; he is given seventy-two black-eyed women; he vouches for seventy of his family to be accepted to paradise..."

Sheik Isma'il Aal Ghadwan, August 17, 2001
(Weekly televised sermon from Gaza)

For Israel, one of the most shocking dimensions of the Intifada was the violent involvement of Palestinian children. As the Intifada progressed, it became clear that not only were Israeli children being deliberately targeted, but that an entire generation of young Palestinians—the same young people who were supposed to grow into Israel's peaceful neighbors—were being educated and groomed to martyr themselves on the altar of murdering Jews. Indeed, the three-day ceremony following the death of a suicide bomber is called the "martyr's wedding" and is marked by distributing sweets to children who come to congratulate the parents of their dead friends.

"A young man said to me, 'I am 14 years old, and I have four years left before I blow myself up against the Jews.' I said to him, 'Oh son, I ask Allah to give you and myself in martyrdom. Blessings for whoever has raised his sons on the education of Jihad and martyrdom. Blessings for whoever has saved a bullet in order to stick it in a Jew's head."

Sheik Ibrahim Madhi, August 3, 2001
(Weekly televised sermon from Gaza)

"I am proud, so proud. I will give all of my children, if that's what it takes to get our homeland back. All of them can become martyrs. It will be a dignity to me."

Afaf Abutayah, mother of a fifteen-year-old boy
killed in a clash with Israeli soldiers,
quoted in the *New York Times*, December 24, 2000

"I am very happy and proud of what my son did, and frankly, a bit jealous. My son has fulfilled the Prophet's [Mohammed's] wishes. Tell me, what more could a father ask?"

Hassan Hotari, whose son blew himself up,
killing twenty-one Israeli teenagers and seriously
wounding many others, quoted in *USA Today*, June 25, 2001

Some Paradigms Shift, Others Crash and Burn

Israel trusted Yasir Arafat.

It trusted that he genuinely accepted Israel's right to exist, that he was prepared to make compromises for the long-term good of his people, and that he would be able to inspire his people with a vision that would make compromise and peace possible.

This trust required a complete reversal for Israelis, but it made the Oslo peace process possible. After Camp David and the Al-Aksa Intifada, it's hard to imagine that such trust can ever be restored.

> *"We had dreams of Israeli and Palestinian children playing together, laughing together. Yes, it is with a heavy heart that we say that our dreams of peace have gone up in the smoke of ransacked synagogues, in the lynching of Israeli prisoners and of blood-thirsty mobs shouting their version of Jerusalem without Jews; and a Middle East without Israel. And I blame the supreme leader of the Palestinians, Yasir Arafat. All his promises were lies; all his commitments were false. I accuse him of murdering the hopes of an entire generation. His and ours."*
> Eli Wiesel, October 12, 2000

An oft-repeated truism about peace agreements is, "You only make peace with your enemies." This is true, but misleading. Of course one only makes peace with an enemy, but not if you think your enemy still desires your demise and looks at "peace" as a way to strengthen his position.

Israel currently finds itself in a terribly difficult position. The pre-Oslo situation was a nightmare, the post-Camp David Intifada is a nightmare, Yasir Arafat is a nightmare, and Hamas is worse. Despite everything, Israelis, and Jews the world over, continue to yearn for peace. Today, the dream of peace is rooted in the hope that somehow Hamas will cease to be a factor, that a new kind of Palestinian leadership will emerge that can nurture a spirit of amicable coexistence in its people and lead them to peace, or that Yasir Arafat himself will miraculously become that leader.

As of the writing of this book, the people of Israel continue to hope and pray for peace—and to fight for their lives, and their home.

The land of Israel.

the holy *Land*

III

heart of the people, soul of *the Nation*

7

"*It is impossible for the Jewish nation to realize its potential except in the chosen land… it is the most precious of all lands, flowing with milk and honey, and its air makes the soul wise.*"
Biblical commentary of R. Isaac Abarbanel, Spanish scholar, rabbinical leader, and financial advisor to Ferdinand and Isabella

Israel and the Essence of the Jewish People

To fully appreciate what Israel is all about, it is imperative to understand its place in the broader context of Judaism and the meaning of Jewish existence. As we will see, the land of Israel is not merely a spiritual luxury item for the Jewish people, but a vital and indispensable dimension of Jewish life, without which the Jewish people cease to be what we are intended to be.

This chapter will begin with a survey of the classical foundations of Judaism. Taken together, these concepts burnish the lens through which Jews have always viewed themselves, the world around them, and their place in the world. With these ideas serving as our cognitive context, we will move on to a look at the ultimate meaning of Israel.

Israel and the Grand Context

In 1947, Rabbis Yitzchak Meir Levin and Moshe Porush made the following statement to the United Nations representatives, when the partition of Palestine and the founding of the State of Israel was being discussed:

> *"We must first declare that which the entire Jewish people agree upon: Eretz Yisrael [the Land of Israel] and the Jewish people are bound to one another forever... This historic event must bring home to every Jew the realization that the Almighty has brought this about in an act of Divine Providence which presents us with a great task, and a grave test. We must face up to this test and establish our life as a people upon the basis of Torah. We are sorely grieved that the land has been divided and sections of the Holy Land have been torn asunder, especially Jerusalem, the Holy City. While we still yearn for the aid of our righteous Messiah, who will bring us total redemption, we nevertheless see the Hand of Providence offering us the opportunity to prepare for the complete redemption, if we will walk into the future as God's people."*

One has to ask, "What were these guys talking about?" What did they mean when they said things like, "The Land of Israel and the Jewish people are bound to one another forever?" And what was all this talk about "Divine Providence," "a great test," a "holy city," and a "walk into the future as God's people?" Such talk sounds more like it belongs in Sunday school than it does at UN deliberations. But these were serious men, and they felt compelled—if they were to speak to the world on behalf of the Jewish people—to dispense with diplomatic jargon in favor of what they understood to be the plain truth. In 1947, the smoldering ashes of millions of Jews still covered across the European continent, and beleaguered survivors were now joining the visionaries who had settled in Israel over the centuries and decades prior to the war. The eyes of Jews everywhere—and indeed the eyes of the entire world—were locked on the vision of an ancient people's return to its ancient homeland.

This statement reflected within it a grand paradigm of life, the world, and history as viewed through the lens of Judaism. Without an understanding of that paradigm, of that overarching Jewish view of life, the statement is simply nonsense.

God's High Hopes

The Jewish Nation is a nation with a mission, and to understand Judaism and Israel it is imperative to understand that mission. In a nutshell, here's the story behind the mission.

A long, long time ago, God created the world, and He had very high hopes for His creation. God had high hopes for the trees and the clouds, for the birds and the beasts, and most of all for human beings. When it came to human beings, God's plan looked like this: He would give people the freedom and ability to make of life, and the world, whatever they wanted. Mankind would be free to create a heaven on earth or a hell on earth. If the world became heaven on earth, people and God would all love to be a part of it and if it became hell on earth, people would be terrified to bring children into it.

While God had His high hopes, things didn't go very well. Starting with Adam and Eve's blunder in the Garden of Eden, a flood of Biblical proportions, and a construction project in Babel gone awry—for one reason or another—mankind just wasn't progressing the way God had hoped. Then one day it happened. A unique individual arose who possessed within himself the potential to lead mankind toward the fulfillment of its enormous potential. This man was Abraham. Abraham was a person who was able to see through the stifling dogmas of his time and make a clean break with the prevailing pagan norms—he was truly one of a kind.

The Mission: God and Abraham Strike a Deal

God wasn't about to let a historic opportunity slip through His fingers, and so He initiated a remarkable relationship with Abraham.

> *"And God said to Abraham; 'Go for yourself and leave your land, the community of your birth, your father's home and head for the land that I will show you. And I will transform you into a great nation and I will bless you—and blessing and goodness will come to all the families of the earth, through you."*
>
> Genesis 12:1-3

> *"And Abraham was ninety-nine years old when God appeared*

to him and said, 'I am the ultimate force in creation; walk before me and represent me with integrity. And I will set my Covenant between Me and between you... as well as your descendants after you, forever..."

Genesis 17:1-2

In Abraham, God saw the makings of the person who had the ability to raise a family that would one day grow into a nation—a nation capable of becoming a beacon of enlightenment for all the families and nations of the earth.

"This covenant imposed binding obligations on both parties involved. Abraham herein committed himself to becoming God's partner in both the repairing of creation and moving it to its final destiny."

Malbim, 19th-century Biblical commentator

One Man, One Family, One Nation

Together, God and Abraham planted the seeds that would eventually reveal the beauty of a long lost garden. But first those seeds had to take root and grow. And grow they did. From Abraham and his wife Sarah there came a family, and eventually, from that family came a nation—the nation of Israel.

Four hundred years after Abraham and Sarah, and after a century of Jewish slavery in Egypt, God offered the Torah to the Jewish people at Mount Sinai. What transpired at Mount Sinai was the national ratification of the original Covenant with Abraham.

"In the third month after the exodus of the Jews from Egypt, on this day, they came to the wilderness of Sinai... And Moses ascended to God and God called to him from the mountain and told him what to say to [Abraham's descendants] the house of Jacob and the children of Israel... And the entire nation gave a united answer, and they said, 'Everything which God has spoken, we will do.'"

Exodus 19:1-8

"I am God; I called you for the purpose of righteousness ...

and I made you a Covenant people, to be a light to the nations."

Isaiah 42:6

"The purpose of creation could not be fulfilled until the Jewish nation left Egypt and received the Torah at Sinai. It was then that they would achieve the potential for being a 'light to the nations' and bring an awareness of God to the entire world."
Rabbi Naftali Tzvi Yehuda Berlin, *Introduction to Exodus*

Israel: There's No Place Like Home

"God made an assessment of every land and found no land more suited to the Jewish people than the land of Israel, and no people more suited to the land of Israel, than the people of Israel."

Midrash, Leviticus Rabbah, 13

After receiving the Torah at Sinai, God instructed Moses to take the Jewish people directly to the land of Israel where they would set up shop and fulfill their mission. The question is this: Why does fulfillment of the Jewish mission require that the Jews live in Israel? The answer lies in understanding that the land of Israel is far more than a mere geographic location on the globe. Just as every human being has a soul—a wellspring from which its spirituality flows—the world too has a soul, and that soul is the land of Israel.

The purpose of creation will be actualized when God's presence in the world is clear to all mankind, and Israel is the place that was custom-designed to facilitate that awareness. For this reason, Israel, the land that is naturally conducive to awareness of God, provides the ideal setting for the people whose mission it is to make that awareness manifest. Like the inspiring beauty of the seasons and the silent ebb and flow of the ocean tides, the unity of the land of Israel with the people of Israel is intrinsic to a naturally balanced, spiritually conscious world. And, just as reckless tampering with just one species can threaten an entire ecosystem, so too when the bond of the people of Israel to the land of Israel is frayed, the spiritual equilibrium of the entire world hangs in the balance. The land of Israel and the Jewish people are truly a match made in heaven, a match upon which all of creation depends.

Given the enormity of the Jewish mission and its linkage to a particular land, it isn't surprising to find that Jewish literature is filled with references that reflect the deeper meaning of Israel and its centrality to Judaism.

I know that some, or many, of the sources listed below may be unfamiliar.
For this reason, each source is followed by a brief background note.
I hope you find these notes helpful.

"The power resulting from the presence of God's light in the world flows most intensely from His people, and His land ... the Holy Land was established as a place that would educate, and illuminate the world. It was designed as the ideal habitat for the tribes of the Children of Israel."

Rabbi Yehuda HaLevi,
twelfth century scholar, philosopher and poet.

"God carefully matched the Jewish nation with a place that complements the nature of Jewish peoplehood. This place is the Land of Israel. Separation of the Jews from the Land of Israel is a complete distortion of Jewish existence."

Rabbi Yehuda Loew, Maharal of Prague
sixteenth century scholar and mystic.

"The land of Israel is dear to Me, and the nation of Israel is dear to Me... I will place the nation of Israel, which is dear to Me, in the land that is dear to Me."

Midrash, Bamidbar Rabbah, 23:7

"The essence of the Torah's commandments is that they be lived and carried out in the land of Israel... the commandments are so deeply linked to the land that their performance anywhere else is almost as if one is just practicing for the day when they can be truly observed."

Nachmanides, a thirteenth century scholar, kabbalist,
and leader of Spanish Jewry. In 1267 he settled in Israel.

"The land of Israel is more than just a means through which the Jewish people are physically unified, strengthened, and religiously inspired... the land is a unique reality profoundly

bound to the deepest essence of the nation of Israel.

The nation of Israel will arise and stand on its own feet, with vitality, in its cherished land. Its life will be a dynamic expression of the prophecy that is at the core of its soul, and it will reinvigorate the seeds of Godliness that are in the heart of all Mankind, and every living being."

R. Avraham Y. Kook, *Orot, Eretz Yisrael, 1; Orot HaTechiya*, 72

Rabbi Kook was a prominent Lithuanian scholar who settled in Israel, where he became the rabbi of Jaffa and then chief rabbi in British Palestine.

"We [in Israel] are able to feel the spiritual effects of the special sanctity of the land of Israel. For example, we see that the study of spiritual, ethical texts has a greater impact on us here... Our sages taught us, 'There is no Torah like the Torah studied in the land of Israel,' and 'The very air of the land of Israel bestows wisdom.' We see clearly that those who study Torah here are able to reach far greater heights than anywhere else."

Rabbi Eliyahu Dessler, *Letters of Eliyahu* 3:194-196

A profound Jewish thinker of the last century, Rabbi Dessler settled in Israel in 1949 and was instrumental in the resurgence of Israeli Torah institutions after the Holocaust.

"What is the unique spiritual quality of the Land of Israel? It seems that it is easier there, more than anywhere else in the world, to form a natural and powerful bond with the Creator... it is not possible to conclude our discussion of Israel without reflecting on an amazing phenomenon, the phenomenon of the Jewish people meriting either to inhabit the land of Israel, or losing the land of Israel, for this phenomenon is the central operative point in all of Jewish history."

Rabbi Shlomo Volbe, *Aley Shur*, 1:284

Rabbi Volbe lives in Jerusalem and is one of Israel's leading sages and most renowned educators.

So there you have it. While it's true that a computer, a monitor, and a keyboard are usually three separate components, ask anyone you meet to picture a computer and they will always think of the three together. Because these components are so fundamentally interdependent in terms of the computer being able to serve its purpose, it's as if the three are really one. Similarly, just as it is impossible to conceive of the Jewish people independent of the Torah—that which is the source of all things Jewish—and just as it is impossible to grasp the full meaning of the Jewish people outside of the context of a mission-centered covenant with God, it is similarly impossible to properly understand the Jewish people as distinct from the land of Israel. In essence, they are all one.

Next Year in Jerusalem

Jerusalem occupies a place in the life of the Jewish people so utterly unique that it defies description. In a way, describing Jerusalem is like describing a sunset—it can't be done. All that one can do is hope to convey something of the drama and the awe stirred by the sunset and then stand back and hope that somehow one heart has touched another. So too Jerusalem. You don't describe it, you emote it...

> *Jerusalem is a prayer and a dream. Its late-night echoes are the melodies of a hundred generations, of yesterday and eternity. Its stone-hard walls are a soft and aged embrace. Jerusalem isn't a place at all—it's she, it's us, it's simplicity. It's a vessel, a corridor, a light. It's everything. A holy whisper and an unfathomable aching for peace. It's God's dew-covered garden path, and something to never be forgotten.*

Of course, this begs a question. What is it about Jerusalem that makes it what it is to the Jewish heart and soul, to Judaism, and to the Jewish people?

To get a sense of what it is that has propelled Jerusalem to the forefront of Jewish consciousness, we will take a look at two things. First, at the place Jerusalem occupies in Jewish life, and second, at the place it occupies in Jewish thought. We'll begin with Jewish life.

Spiritual Compass

Almost every synagogue in the world is built to face Jerusalem, and when Jews have prayed, no matter where they were on the face of the earth, they always turned and prayed toward Jerusalem.

Daily Prayers and Blessings

The following words are a part of the Jews' daily prayers: *"And to Jerusalem Your city, return in mercy, and dwell in it as You have proclaimed. And build it, soon, in our days—an eternal building."* And, in the blessings at the conclusion of a meal, Jews recite, *"Blessed are You God, for the land, and for the sustenance... And build Jerusalem, the holy city, soon in our days."*

Passover Seder

No matter where they happened to be eating their matzah, Jews conclude the seder with the words, "Next Year in Jerusalem."

Under the Chuppah

Special blessings recited at a Jewish wedding include the words: *"There will yet again be heard in the cities of Judah, and in the courtyards of Jerusalem, the voice of celebration and joy—the voice of the groom and the bride."*

Circumcision

A widespread Sephardic (belonging to Jews of Mediterranean descent) custom at the *brit mila* (circumcision ceremony) is for the father of the baby to lead all the guests in reciting the verse, *"If I forget thee Jerusalem, may my right hand lose its strength..."* A *brit mila* marks the continuity of the original covenant between God and Abraham to each new baby and each new generation.

A New Home

When Jews build or acquire a new home, there is a custom to leave a portion of the interior unpainted. Why? So that even in the comfort of home, they never forget that a Jewish home is incomplete while Jerusalem is in ruins.

Yom Kippur

For century upon century, every synagogue's Yom Kippur service has concluded with the same words as the Passover seder, "Next Year in Jerusalem."

Transcendent Inspiration

It's been thousands of years since the Jewish people were sovereign in Israel and since Jerusalem was their capital. And somehow, some way, not only did the Jewish people never forget Jerusalem and not only did they long for "Next Year in Jerusalem," but it actually became a reality.

Consider this:

On July 14, 1978, Anatoly (Natan) Sharansky stood before a

Soviet court about to sentence him to fifteen years in prison for crimes like studying Hebrew, learning about Judaism, and wanting to emigrate to Israel, and said,

"For 2,000 years the Jewish people, my people, have been dispersed all over the world and seemingly deprived of any hope of returning. But still, each year Jews have stubbornly, and apparently without reason, said to each other, '*L'shana ha'bah b'Yirusholayim*, Next Year in Jerusalem.' And today, when I am further than ever from my dream, from my people, and from my [wife] Avital, and when many difficult years of prison and camps lie ahead of me, I say to my wife and to my people, *L'shana ha'baah b'Yirusholayim*—Next Year in Jerusalem."

Today, Anatoly Sharansky lives in Israel with his wife and children, and is a member of the Israeli Parliament.

Jewish life is thus animated by connections to Jerusalem at almost every turn, and the same is true for Jewish thought. Let's take a look.

Holy Dust

According to tradition, an outcropping of bedrock on the Temple Mount is the spot from which God began creation. Further, when the Torah says that the first human beings were created "from the dust of the earth," it means the dust from the Temple Mount. Finally, when the Jewish people were instructed to build the Temple in Jerusalem, they built it on this very same spot. The Temple in Jerusalem was always understood to be not only central to the relationship between God and the Jewish people but also vital to the connection between God and all mankind.

Abraham Hits the Road

The primary events in Abraham's life revolved around a series of ten tests. At the center of both Abraham's first and last test was a journey to Israel. The first test was introduced with God saying the following to Abraham, "**You should leave and go** *out on your own; leave your land, the place of your birth, and your father's house, and go to the land that I will show you*" (Genesis 12:1). Later, before the tenth and final test, God said, "*Take your son, your only son, the one you love, Isaac, and,* **you should leave and go** *to the land of Moriah*" (Genesis 22:2). In the first test, God's unnamed destination was Israel, and in the last test it was the plateau that is the heart of Jerusalem—the Temple Mount.

Let's All Go to Jerusalem

When the Temple stood in Jerusalem, there was a special obligation for the Jewish people to gather there for the festivals of Passover, Shavuot, and Sukkot. Imagine the scene, and imagine the feeling. As the festivals approached, hundreds of thousands of families would pack up and go to Jerusalem to celebrate the holidays. There, together with virtually all their fellow Jews, they would assemble for celebration, for study, and for inspiration. Three times a year, in the most tangible and spiritually focused way possible, Jerusalem would become the experiential center of every Jew's life.

The Ninth of Av

For over two thousand years, Jews, wherever they were, have gathered together on the Ninth of Av to mourn the destruction of Jerusalem and the burning of the Temples.

There is a story told about Napoleon Bonaparte and the Ninth of Av:

Once, Napoleon and his entourage were riding past a synagogue in Paris when they heard a terrible wailing coming from inside the building. Napoleon had his officers investigate, and they reported that the Jews were all sitting on the floor of the synagogue and crying over the destruction of Jerusalem. Napoleon is said to have commented that any people that can mourn its loss for so many centuries will certainly live to see its city rebuilt.

Stairway to Heaven

"And Jacob left Beersheva and he arrived at a certain place, and went to sleep. And he dreamed and saw a ladder that was standing firmly on the ground, though it reached all the way to heaven... And God was present, and said, 'I am God. The God of Abraham your father, and the God of Isaac. I will give the land that you are lying on to you, and to your descendants.' And Jacob awoke suddenly from his sleep, and he said, 'This place is truly wondrous; this must be nothing less than God's abode, and the gateway to the heavens.'"

Genesis 28:16-17

The place where Jacob slept was none other than the Temple Mount. In Jewish thought, Jerusalem is the spiritual epicenter of the universe—it is "the gateway to heaven." Judaism has always insisted that intimate connection to God is available to all people, in all places.

It's just that from anywhere other than Jerusalem, it's like going up a down escalator. In Jerusalem, the elevator is always going up; all you have to do is get on.

The Prayer of Moses

Perhaps nothing better highlights the spiritual significance of the land of Israel, and of Jerusalem, than a prayer uttered by Moses himself near the end of his life. At that point, the only thing lacking in Moses' resume was the experience of entering the land of Israel—and this was an experience that God told him he would never have.

Now let's consider the prayer of Moses:

Moses, having scaled the greatest heights of knowledge and closeness to God, still wanted to go higher. He wanted even greater awareness and a deeper, more intimate connection to God. And so, at the threshold of the land of Israel, Moses prayed.

> *"You have just begun to show your servant Your greatness, and Your powerful hand; for what force is there in the heaven or on the earth that can do anything like your mighty deeds. Please let me go over and see the good land that is on the other side of the Jordan, this good mountain, and the Lebanon."*
>
> Deuteronomy 3:24

> *"The 'good land' is referring to the land of Israel, the 'good mountain' is Jerusalem, and the 'Lebanon' is the Temple in Jerusalem ."*
>
> Commentary of Rashi, Deuteronomy 3:24

Moses knew that everything he so deeply longed for was attainable only in the land of Israel. He also knew that, beyond Israel in general, what he longed for was even more intensely accessible in Jerusalem and, more intensely still, in the Temple that was destined to stand as the spiritual epicenter of the world.

> *"Moses wasn't driven to enter Israel in order to taste its fruits; rather, it was because it is a land that was established for the purpose of unusually elevated sanctity, and there he would be able to achieve the greatest spiritual heights."*
>
> Commentary of Malbim, Deuteronomy 3:24

Exile Ends, Mission Accomplished

While the Torah saw the potential for exile, it also foresaw the inevitability of a Jewish return to Israel and Jerusalem. And it saw the day, after the return, when the awareness of God would become brilliantly manifest in Jerusalem.

> *"Even if the dispersed among you will be at the end of the heavens; your God will take you, and gather you from there. And God will bring you to the land that your forefathers possessed, and you will possess it; and He will do good for you, and you will flourish even more than your forefathers."*
>
> Deuteronomy 30:1-5

> *"So said God: I have returned to Zion, and I have made My dwelling within Jerusalem. And I will bring them and they will dwell within Jerusalem; and they will be to Me a nation, and I will be to them God; in truth and righteousness."*
>
> Zechariah, 8:3-8

Israel: The Grand Context Revisited

It's now time to look again at the statement made by Rabbis Yitzchak Meir Levin and Moshe Porush, the Agudat Israel representatives to the United Nations in 1947, and to consider its meaning and implications in light of Judaism's bigger picture.

> *We must first declare that which the entire Jewish people agree upon: Eretz Yisrael [the Land of Israel] and the Jewish people are bound to one another forever... This historic event must bring home to every Jew the realization that the Almighty has brought this about in an act of Divine Providence which presents us with a great task, and a grave test. We must face up to this test and establish our life as a people upon the basis of Torah. We are sorely grieved that the land has been divided and sections of the Holy Land have been torn asunder, especially Jerusalem, the Holy City. While we still yearn for the aid of our righteous Messiah, who will bring us total redemption, we nevertheless see the Hand of Providence offering us the opportunity to prepare for the complete redemption, if we will walk into the future as God's people.*

With an appreciation of the seminal concepts that shape Jewish consciousness, it becomes clear that what we have here is a statement that powerfully reflects a grand paradigm that includes the covenantal relationship between God and the significance of the land of Israel. Let's take another look.

> **We must first declare that which the entire Jewish people agree upon: Eretz Yisrael [the Land of Israel] and the Jewish people are bound to one another forever.**

What chutzpah! After World War I, the land of Israel passed from Turkish rule to the hands of the British. Then, after World War II, the nations of the world sat at the United Nations to deliberate about what to do with the land then called Palestine. And what do these rabbis have to say (in the most polite and diplomatic way they can)? "Sorry folks, but the truth is that Israel always has, and always will be, the homeland of the Jewish people. God gave it to us, the Babylonians and the Romans stole it, subsequent powers inherited stolen goods, and now—to be honest—all you are deliberating about is the efficacy of returning to us that which is ours in the first place."

> **This historic event must bring home to every Jew the realization that the Almighty has brought this about in an act of Divine Providence...**

So what was all this Divine Providence stuff supposed to mean? Clearly what they were saying was this: Events that take place in world history are not coincidences and are not only the result of the decisions and policies of men. Rather, when it comes to human history, the Creator of the universe has a hands-on policy. After two thousand years of dispersion, it was obvious that the reestablishment of Jewish sovereignty in Israel was a part of God's larger intentions for the Jewish people.

> **...which presents us with a great task, and a grave test. We must face up to this test and establish our life as a people upon the basis of Torah.**

The establishment of the State of Israel is both a divine gift, and a divine challenge of the highest order. The challenge is to bring the land

and the people together in the only way that can possibly result in the fulfillment of what their heavenly union is all about in the first place. This fulfillment will only come about via a full and vibrant actualization of Jewish life lived by the Jewish people in the Jewish homeland. And if Jewish life is anything at all, it is the life whose blueprint is the Torah. In other words, the task at hand in the land of Israel was—and is—the emergence of a beautifully flourishing national life that is informed and guided in the deepest and broadest sense by the wisdom and precepts of God's Torah.

> **We are sorely grieved that the land has been divided and sections of the Holy Land have been torn asunder, especially Jerusalem, the Holy City.**

For the land of Israel to be in the hands of foreign powers is a source of deep anguish for the Jewish people. As for Jerusalem, for her to be "torn asunder" as she was by partition, and for Jews to have to see the precious Temple Mount and the Western Wall abused by Arab overlords, was profoundly distressing.

> **While we still yearn for the aid of our righteous Messiah, who will bring us total redemption, we nevertheless see the Hand of Providence offering us the opportunity to prepare for the complete redemption, if we will walk into the future as God's people.**

What we have here is nothing less than a vision of God's Covenant with the Jewish people achieving its ultimate fulfillment. The Jewish vision of the future is one in which the entire Jewish nation—led by an exceptional personality—will return to the land of Israel, fully embrace its relationship with God, rebuild the Temple in Jerusalem, and finally fulfill the mission of being the conduit through which God's light and blessing will flow to all mankind.

So That's What They Meant

To Jews who looked at life through the lens of Judaism, it was almost impossible to relate to the reestablishment of Jewish sovereignty in Israel as anything less than one of Jewish history's definitive events, albeit an event that was a work in progress. Then, in June of 1967 when the Israeli Defense Forces liberated the Temple Mount and the Western

Wall, Jews everywhere were thunderstruck. The return of the Jewish people to Israel, and now to Jerusalem, were events without parallel in all of human history. These were events that carried within them the echoes of God's Covenant with Abraham and of two millennia of prayer and anticipation. Finally, the time had arrived when the people of Israel would be united with the land of Israel, and in that reunion, they expected to achieve the ultimate union of the people of Israel with the God of Abraham, Isaac, and Jacob—the God of Israel.

One Shavuot in Jerusalem

Shavuot is the holiday that celebrates the receiving of the Torah at Sinai, and is one of the three festivals during which Jews made a pilgrimage to Jerusalem in the days of the Temple. There is a widespread custom to stay up the entire night of Shavuot studying Torah texts, and to recite the morning prayers at sunrise. Today, tens of thousands of people gather at the Western Wall on Shavuot morning for these special sunrise services. The following is one man's account of Shavuot morning at the Wall, one week after it was liberated from the Jordanians in 1967.

If we waited for years, yearning for the day when we could stand at the Kotel Ha-ma'aravi [the Western Wall], the relic of our holy Temple, there to express our overflowing emotions in whispered prayer before the Creator—in the last few days the anticipation became immeasurably more intense. We even began to count the hours remaining till the moment when the way would be open to the mass of visitors.

At last we set out for the Old City, at the early morning hour, in the hope that there would not yet be any great press of people. But once we stepped out into the street, we realized how wrong we were. The street was humming with people. From every side and corner a stream of people came pouring in. And from all the roads they flowed into a mighty river of humanity coursing toward Mount Zion. All roads and paths led to the Kotel, and spontaneously people burst into spirited singing and dancing. We saw soldiers amongst Chassidim, old mixed with young, European westernized Ashkenazim, and oriental Sephardim. Who noticed differences or distinctions? All barriers fell, became null and void, as though they had never been.

On we marched in that throng of enthusiasm, utterly amazed and wondering: Were we really going to the Kotel? Was it only a week since we sat in shelters and prayed to the Creator to save us from the killers who planned to exterminate us?

The long twisting line of people has reached the Kotel at last. At first glance it is just an ordinary wall of huge hard stones. Yet it expresses so very much; it "speaks" to you with such eloquence; and in truth, it seems to listen. We stood there dumbfounded, all speech taken from us. Hot tears poured unashamedly from the worshipers' eyes everywhere, without restraint...

With a kiss for those great stones, we leave the Wall and turn back, homeward-bound. On the way back you could see again all the barriers down, fallen between Jew and fellow Jew. We witnessed expressions of affection and friendship that we had never seen before.

Isaac J. Hershkovitz, June 1967, from *The Western Wall*

Going on Sixty

"In Israel, in order to be a realist, you have to believe in miracles."

David Ben-Gurion, first Prime Minister of Israel

The re-establishment of the Jewish people in our homeland has now entered its sixth decade. If Israel is anything, it is a miracle. In barely fifty years, and despite the relentless efforts of enemies who would like nothing better than to see Israel destroyed and its Jews slaughtered, the impossible has happened. Israel has become a thriving and sophisticated modern society, and has begun to bring the Jewish people together in a way that hasn't existed for over twenty-five hundred years. In the midst of the daunting task of building a democratic society from scratch, Israel has successfully absorbed millions of Jews from all over the world, including concentration camp survivors from Europe; refugees from Iraq, Iran, Yemen, and Egypt; idealists from the United States, Canada, and Australia; persecuted Jews from Ethiopia; and hundreds of thousands from the former Soviet Union. Israel has become one of the world's leading exporters of fruits, flowers, and diamonds; its high-tech industry rivals Silicon Valley; it is home to great universities, research centers, and hospitals; and it has become the reborn spiritual center of the Jewish people. Israel is now Jewry's preeminent center of Torah study and the home of our greatest Torah academies for the first time in almost two thousand years.

At the same time, even with all that has been achieved, it seems that Israel is still an unfolding potentiality that has yet to be fully realized, and a soaring opportunity that has yet to be fully embraced.

Where Does That Leave Us ?

Let's consider the words of Rabbi Yehuda Halevi in his classic work on Jewish thought, the Kuzari. Likewise, it will be informative to consider the context in which these words were written and the man who wrote them.

Yehuda Halevi lived in Spain at a time when Israel was being ravaged by the Crusades, and when living conditions for the tiny remnant of Jews in Israel were as dangerous and desperate as they had ever been. Nonetheless, in the year 1145, Halevi left the comforts of Spanish life behind to set out on what would become a legendary five-year journey to settle in Israel.

Now for the words of Rabbi Yehuda Halevi:

"Despite all that we know about the precious spiritual status of the land of Israel, still, we have failed to make this place the focus of our life's goals. And, it is this very shortcoming that prevented us from grasping the historic opportunity that existed during the era of the Second Temple. With the beginning of the rebuilding of the Second Temple, and the initial return of thousands of Jews to Israel, God was making it clear that He was prepared to restore all of the spiritual grandeur that had existed prior to the destruction—if only the entire people had been profoundly desirous to return home. However, only a minority returned, while the majority, including the leadership, remained in Babylon, where they preferred to live in exile in the comfort of their homes and worldly possessions. This is what is meant by the verse in Song

of Songs, 'I am asleep but my heart is awake.' Exile is a deep sleep, and while in our heart of hearts there is a longing to return to Israel, it is difficult to stir ourselves from the depths of our slumber."

Where does the existence of Israel leave us today, and what are the implications for a generation to whom a life in Israel is so accessible? It seems that today we Jews stand confronted. At the very least, it appears as if the Divine Hand in history is once again stretched out to us, and therefore we have to ask ourselves, Do we truly long to return home? Do we shudder at the thought of seeing our children and grandchildren raised on exile's foreign soil? Do we dream of being able to walk with our friends and family through the streets of Jerusalem, Safed, Tel Aviv, and Hebron, or are we perfectly content in New York, Toronto, Chicago, and London? Do we feel that life is okay just the way it is, or do we anxiously look forward to a sea change—to a time when the Jewish people will return to Israel and achieve everything inherent in our eternal Covenant with God?

These words, spoken to the UN representatives in 1947 still echo in our ears:

*This historic event must bring home to every Jew
the realization that the Almighty has brought this about
in an act of Divine Providence,
which presents us with a great task,
and a grave test.*

epilogue:
Of Dreams, and Prayers,
and Miracles

Of Dreams ...

"When God brings about the return to Zion [Jerusalem], we will have been like dreamers."

King David, *Book of Psalms*, 126

Twenty-eight hundred years ago, King David painted a picture of what was then the distant future. There, in the dawning days of the First Temple era, somehow David sensed what the crescendo of history would feel like. When the Jewish people would finally return to Zion, David knew that we would all feel "like dreamers."

The question is: What does that mean? Some say that when we return to Zion the pain of two thousand years of exile will suddenly vanish, and it will feel like waking up from an awful nightmare. Others say that when we return to Zion it will feel like a long-awaited dream come true.

I suspect that both are correct. Indeed, the return of the Jewish people to Zion will be a dream come true—a dream whose magnificent realization will be so overwhelming that everything we endured during the long night of exile will seem like little more than a bad dream.

... and Prayers

"For out of Zion will come the teachings of the Torah, and the word of God from Jerusalem. And He will judge between many peoples, and settle the disputes of powerful nations, even those that are far away. They will beat their swords into

plowshares and their spears into pruning knives; nation shall not lift up sword against nation, and they will not learn war anymore."

Micah 4:2-4

"A new light will shine upon Zion. May we all soon merit to benefit from this light."

Daily prayer book

We Jews have always been dreamers; and we have always prayed that our dreams come true. For millennia we prayed, "Next Year in Jerusalem"; and then our dream came true. We prayed for our brothers and sisters in Ethiopia and behind the Iron Curtain, that they too would be able to return home. And our dream came true. Today we pray for peace, and for the realization of our greatest dream—a dream for all mankind.

... and Miracles

On August, 9, 2001 Malki Roth, aged 15, and her friend Michal Raziel were having lunch at Sbarro in Jerusalem. While Malki and Michal were enjoying their pizza, a suicide bomber walked in and blew himself and half the people in Sbarro to pieces. The next day, Malki and Michal were buried next to one another.

I visited the Roth family during the seven-day mourning period known as *shiva*. Before I left the house, Arnold Roth, Malki's father, asked that I take two messages with me—one from him, and one from Malki. Arnold Roth said, "Tell the Jews of America that we love it here. Tell them life is beautiful here. Tell them to come, to visit, to join us." And then he handed me a magazine article written by Malki in 1997. He told me he sensed that, through this article, Malki was speaking to all of us. He asked that I pay particular attention to the last paragraph. I did, and I still do. This is what she wrote:

> *"In conclusion, I want to say to all of you*
> *that are reading this right now:*
> *You are not allowed to lose your hope,*
> *because maybe a miracle will happen.*
> *DO NOT LOSE HOPE!"*

a map is worth a thousand

Words

Israel and the Arab World

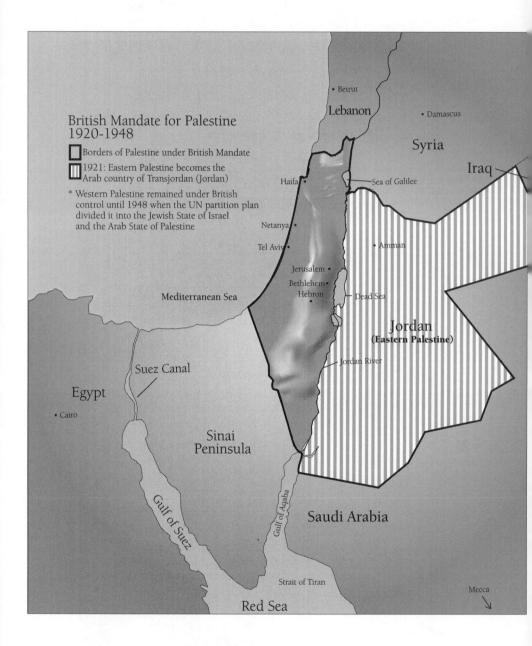

British Mandate for Palestine 1920-1948

Borders of Palestine under British Mandate

1921: Eastern Palestine becomes the Arab country of Transjordan (Jordan)

* Western Palestine remained under British control until 1948 when the UN partition plan divided it into the Jewish State of Israel and the Arab State of Palestine

• Beirut

Lebanon

• Damascus

Syria

Iraq

Haifa •

Sea of Galilee

Netanya •

Tel Aviv •

• Amman

Jerusalem •

Bethlehem •

Hebron •

Dead Sea

Mediterranean Sea

Jordan
(Eastern Palestine)

Jordan River

Suez Canal

Egypt

• Cairo

Sinai
Peninsula

Gulf of Suez

Gulf of Aqaba

Saudi Arabia

Strait of Tiran

Mecca

Red Sea

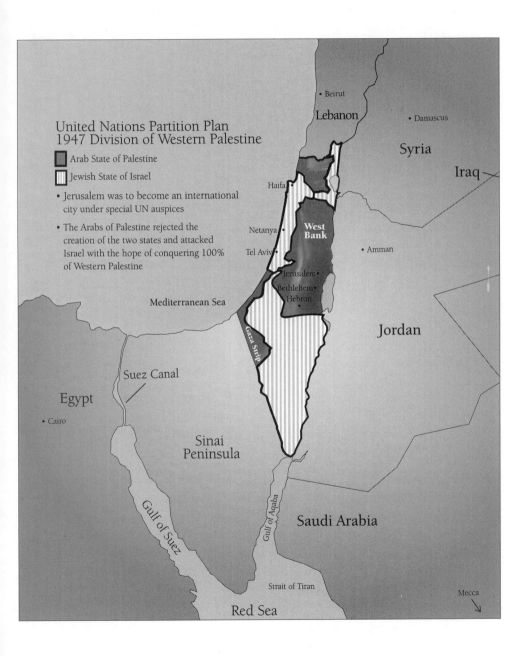

United Nations Partition Plan
1947 Division of Western Palestine

■ Arab State of Palestine

▥ Jewish State of Israel

• Jerusalem was to become an international
city under special UN auspices

• The Arabs of Palestine rejected the
creation of the two states and attacked
Israel with the hope of conquering 100%
of Western Palestine

Beirut
Lebanon
• Damascus
Syria
Iraq
Haifa
West Bank
Netanya
Tel Aviv
• Amman
Jerusalem
Bethlehem
Hebron
Mediterranean Sea
Gaza Strip
Jordan
Suez Canal
Egypt
• Cairo
Sinai Peninsula
Gulf of Suez
Gulf of Aqaba
Saudi Arabia
Strait of Tiran
Mecca
Red Sea

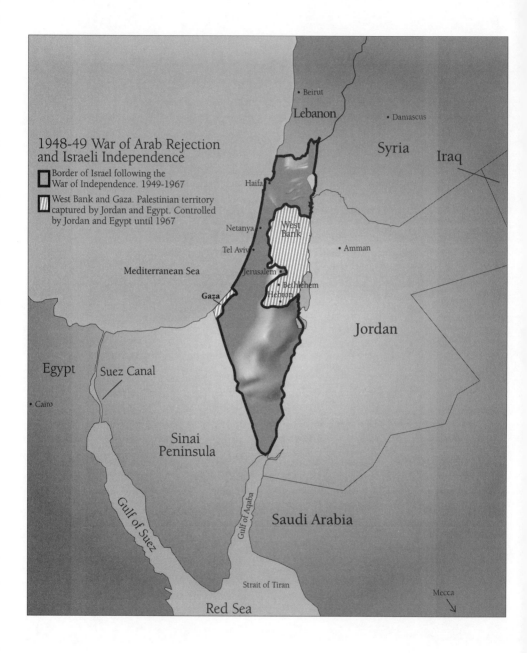

1948-49 War of Arab Rejection
and Israeli Independence

Border of Israel following the
War of Independence. 1949-1967

West Bank and Gaza. Palestinian territory
captured by Jordan and Egypt. Controlled
by Jordan and Egypt until 1967

Beirut

Lebanon

Damascus

Syria

Iraq

Haifa

Netanya

West
Bank

Tel Aviv

Amman

Jerusalem

Mediterranean Sea

Bethlehem
Hebron

Gaza

Jordan

Egypt

Suez Canal

Cairo

Sinai
Peninsula

Gulf of Suez

Gulf of Aqaba

Saudi Arabia

Strait of Tiran

Red Sea

Mecca

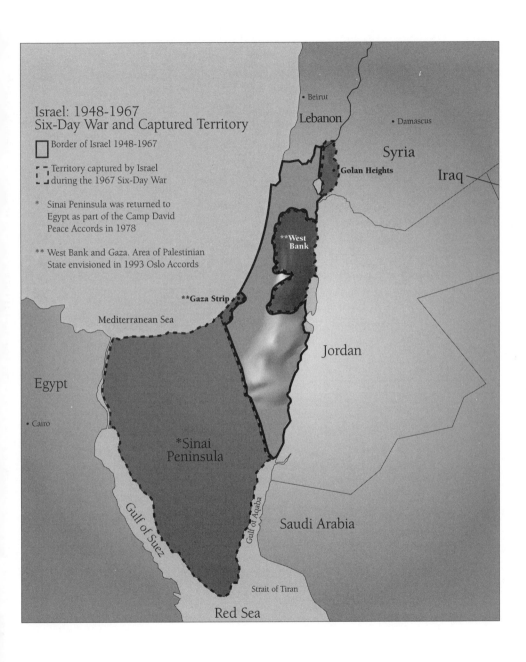

Israel: 1948-1967
Six-Day War and Captured Territory

☐ Border of Israel 1948-1967

⌐ ⌐ Territory captured by Israel
└ ┘ during the 1967 Six-Day War

*   Sinai Peninsula was returned to
    Egypt as part of the Camp David
    Peace Accords in 1978

** West Bank and Gaza. Area of Palestinian
    State envisioned in 1993 Oslo Accords

• Beirut

Lebanon

• Damascus

Syria

Golan Heights

Iraq

**West
Bank

**Gaza Strip

Mediterranean Sea

Jordan

Egypt

• Cairo

*Sinai
Peninsula

Gulf of Suez

Gulf of Aqaba

Saudi Arabia

Strait of Tiran

Red Sea

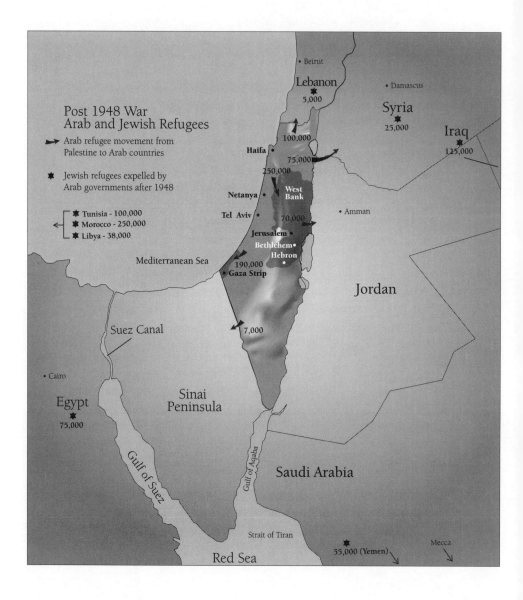

Post 1948 War
Arab and Jewish Refugees

➤ Arab refugee movement from
Palestine to Arab countries

✱ Jewish refugees expelled by
Arab governments after 1948

✱ Tunisia - 100,000
✱ Morocco - 250,000
✱ Libya - 38,000

Mediterranean Sea

Suez Canal

Cairo

Egypt
✱
75,000

Sinai
Peninsula

Gulf of Suez

Gulf of Aqaba

Strait of Tiran

Red Sea

Beirut

Lebanon
✱
5,000

Damascus

Syria
✱
25,000

Iraq
✱
125,000

100,000

Haifa

75,000

250,000

Netanya

West
Bank

Tel Aviv

70,000

Amman

Jerusalem
Bethlehem
Hebron

190,000
Gaza Strip

Jordan

7,000

Saudi Arabia

Mecca

55,000 (Yemen)

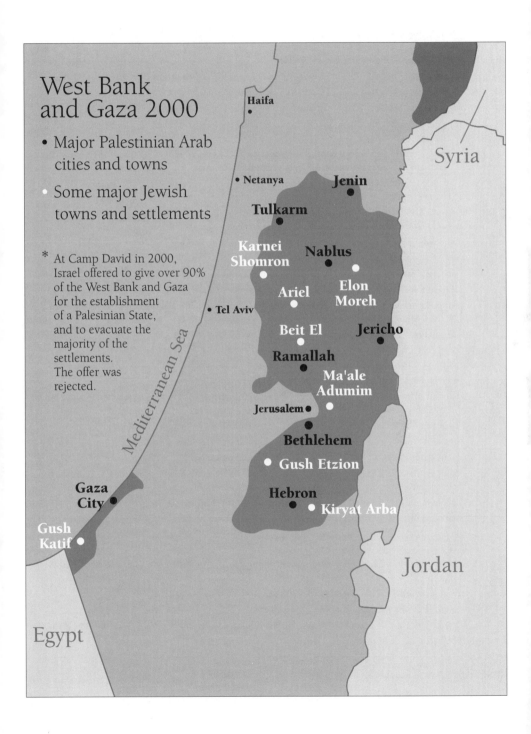

West Bank and Gaza 2000

- Major Palestinian Arab cities and towns
- Some major Jewish towns and settlements

* At Camp David in 2000, Israel offered to give over 90% of the West Bank and Gaza for the establishment of a Palesinian State, and to evacuate the majority of the settlements. The offer was rejected.

Haifa

Syria

Netanya   Jenin

Tulkarm

Karnei Shomron   Nablus

Tel Aviv   Ariel   Elon Moreh

Beit El   Jericho

Ramallah

Ma'ale Adumim

Jerusalem

Bethlehem

Gush Etzion

Hebron

Kiryat Arba

Mediterranean Sea

Gaza City

Gush Katif

Egypt

Jordan

WORKS CITED

Armstrong, Karen. *Jerusalem: One City, Three Faiths*. Ballantine Books, 1997.

Avneri, Arieh L. *The Claim of Land Dispossession: Jewish Land Settlement and the Arabs 1878-1948*. Transaction Books, 1984.

Bard, Mitchell G. *Myths and Facts: A Guide to the Arab-Israeli Conflict*. AICE, 2001.

Bar-Zohar, Michael. *Lionhearts: Heroes of Israel*. Warner books, 1998.

Ben-Sasson, H. H. *A History of the Jewish People*. Harvard University Press, 1976.

Bloom, Jonathan and Blair, Sheila. *Islam: A Thousand Years of Faith and Power*. TV Books, 2000.

Cohen, Amnon and Lewis, Bernard. *Population and Revenue in the Towns of Palestine in the Sixteenth Century*. Princeton University Press, 1978.

Curtis, Michael; Neyer, Joseph; Waxman, Chaim L.; Pollack, Allen. *The Palestinians: People, History, Politics*. American Academic Association for Peace in the Middle East, 1975.

David, Abraham. *To Come to the Land: Immigration and Settlement in Sixteenth Century Eretz-Israel*. University of Alabama Press, 1999.

Emerson, Steven. *American Jihad: The Terrorists Living Among Us*. Free Press, 2002.

Gilbert, Martin. *Israel: A History*. William Morrow, 1998.

Herzog, Chaim. *The Arab-Israeli Wars*. Vintage Books, 1982.

Harkabi, Yehoshafat. *Israel's Fateful Hour*. Harper & Row, 1988.

Hoge, James F. Jr. and Rose, Gideon. *How Did This Happen?: Terrorism and the New Wars*. Public Affairs, 2001.

Idinopulos, Thomas A. *Jerusalem: A History of the Holiest City as Seen Through the Struggles of Jews, Christians, and Muslims*. Ivan R. Dee Elephant Paperback, 1994.

Johnson, Paul. *A History of the Jews*. Harper & Row, 1987.

Kasher, Menahem M. *The Western Wall*. Judaica Press, 1972.

Khalidi, Rashid. *Palestinian Identity: The Construction of Modern Consciousness*. Columbia University Press, 1997.

Laqueur, Walter and Rubin, Barry. *The Israel-Arab Reader*. Penguin Books, 1985.

Lewis, Bernard. *The Arabs in History*. Oxford University Press, 1993.

Mansfield, Peter. *A History of the Middle East*. Penguin Books, 1992.

Morris, Benny. *The Birth of the Palestinian Refugee Problem, 1947-1949*. Cambridge University Press, 1987.

Netanyahu, Benjamin. *Terrorism: How the West Can Win*. Farrar, Strauss and Giroux, 1986.

Parker, James W. *Whose Land? A History of the People of Palestine*. Penguin Books, 1970.

Peters, Joan. *From Time Immemorial: The Origins of the Arab-Israeli Conflict Over Palestine*. Harper & Row, 1984.

Sachar, Howard M. *A History of Israel: From the Rise of Zionism to Our Time*. Alfred A. Knopf, 1996.

Said, Edward W. *The Question of Palestine*. Vintage Books, 1992.

Savir, Uri. *The Process*. Random House, 1998.

Voss, Carl Hermann. *The Palestine Problem Today: Israel and Its Neighbors*. Beacon Press, 1953.

RECOMMENDED BOOKS AND WEB SITES

Ehrlich-Klein, Tzvia. *To Dwell in the Palace: Perspectives on Eretz Yisroel.* Feldheim, 1991.

Fromkin, David. *A Peace to End All Peace: The Fall of the Ottoman Empire and the Creation of the Modern Middle East.* Owl Books, 2001.

Gilbert, Martin. *The Atlas of Jewish History.* William Morrow, 1993.

Katz, Samuel. *Battleground: Fact and Fantasy in Palestine.* Bantam Books, 1973.

Kramer, Elliot M. *A Time For Truth.* 2001.

Laqueur, Walter. *A History of Zionism.* Fine Communications, 1997.

Lewis, Bernard. *What Went Wrong: Western Impact and Middle Eastern Response.* Oxford University Press, 2001.

Netanyahu, Benjamin. *A Place Among the Nations: Israel and the World.* Bantam Books, 1993.

Sachar, Howard M. *Israel and Europe: An Appraisal in History.* Vintage Books, 2000.

Samson, David and Fishman, Tzvi. *Lights on Orot: The Teachings of Harav Avraham Yitzchak Hacohen Kook.* Torat Eretz Yisroel Publications, 2000.

Sela, Avraham. *Political Encyclopedia of the Middle East.* The Jerusalem Publishing House, 1999.

Stein, Kenneth W. *The Land Question in Palestine, 1917-1939.* University of North Carolina Press, 1984.

Vogel, Lester I. *To See A Promised Land: Americans and the Holy Land in the Nineteenth Century.* Pennsylvania State University Press, 1993.

Watt, W. Montgomery. *Muhammad: Prophet and Statesman.* Oxford University Press, 1964.

Wein, Berel. *Faith and Fate: The Story of the Jewish People in the Twentieth Century.* Shaar Press, 2001.

aipac.org (American Israel Public Affairs Committee)

aish.com/jewishissues/middleast

haaretzdaily.com (Israeli daily newspaper)

honestreporting.com

israelbehindthenews.com

israelinsider.com

israelnationalnews.com

jcpa.org (Jerusalem Center for Public Affairs)

jpost.com (Jerusalem Post Newspaper)

memri.org (Middle East Media Research Institute)

pmw.org.il (Palestinian Media Watch)

us-israel.org

walk4israel.com

zoa.org (Zionist Organization of America)

Did you enjoy this book?

Check out other titles in the JUDAISM IN A NUTSHELL series...
JUDAISM IN A NUTSHELL is a growing collection of books designed to make Judaism's most important ideas and issues accessible to people who are *long on curiosity but short on time.*

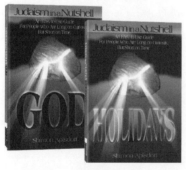

JUDAISM IN A NUTSHELL:
GOD

JUDAISM IN A NUTSHELL:
HOLIDAYS

Other books by Shimon Apisdorf:

ROSH HASHANAH YOM KIPPUR SURVIVAL KIT
by Shimon Apisdorf   1993 Benjamin Franklin Award

PASSOVER SURVIVAL KIT   SURVIVAL KIT FAMILY HAGGADAH
by Shimon Apisdorf   by Shimon Apisdorf

CHANUKAH: *EIGHT NIGHTS OF LIGHT, EIGHT GIFTS FOR THE SOUL*
by Shimon Apisdorf   1997 Benjamin Franklin Award

DEATH OF CUPID   ONE HOUR PURIM PRIMER
by Nachum Braverman   by Shimon Apisdorf
and Shimon Apisdorf